Contents

Chapter 5

PLANNED PREVENTIVE MAINTENANCE 81

Chapter 6

PROCUREMENT AND MANAGEMENT OF CONSULTANCY SERVICES 99

Appendix

USEFUL NAMES AND ADDRESSES 123

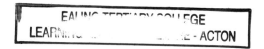
Estate Management in Further Education Colleges

A GOOD PRACTICE GUIDE

Prepared for

The Further Education Funding Council
in association with
the National Audit Office

by

Chesterton International plc

London HMSO

**THE
FURTHER
EDUCATION
FUNDING
COUNCIL**

NAO
NATIONAL AUDIT OFFICE

Chapter 1
INTRODUCTION

The Further Education Funding Council (FEFC) was set up in July 1992 to fund further education in England. The further education sector comprises over 450 colleges, in nine regions of England. The colleges were incorporated as independent bodies in April 1993 and vary widely in terms of student numbers, size, the nature of their activities and the number of sites which they occupy.

The FEFC's expressed aims are:

- to secure throughout England sufficient and adequate facilities for further education to meet the needs of students, including those with learning difficulties and/or disabilities, and the communities in which they live

- to contribute to the development of a highly skilled and competitive workforce particularly as envisaged in the National Training and Education Targets

- to promote improvements in the quality of further education

- to promote access to further education for people who do not participate in education and training but would benefit from it

- to ensure that the achievements, contribution and potential of the sector and its financial needs are properly presented at national level

- to secure value for money for the funds employed by the FEFC.

To contribute towards the aim of securing value for money, the FEFC invited the National Audit Office (NAO) to work with it in promoting a series of value for money studies. These are to be implemented by the FEFC's own audit service and other professional teams in association with the NAO, and will lead to the publication of good practice guides in some key areas of activity undertaken by colleges.

Following an earlier study into purchasing, the FEFC agreed to undertake this study of value for money in estate management practice.

The guidelines that are presented in this report, which do not override any guidance issued or to be issued by the FEFC to the contrary, have been prepared following a study commissioned by the FEFC in November 1994. The FEFC appointed Chesterton International plc to conduct the study and a team from the practice was assisted by the NAO in the fact-finding stages of the assignment.

Throughout the conduct of the study, a significant number of individuals within colleges spent time in discussion with the study team and completing questionnaires. The FEFC and the study team are grateful for the contributions of all participants in the study.

1 DESCRIPTION OF THE GUIDE

1.1   This report, *Estate Management in Further Education Colleges: A Good Practice Guide*, has been prepared to meet a need for an authoritative and practical guide to assist colleges in managing their estates. It is not intended to cover all aspects of estate management, but to concentrate on five key topic areas. The terms of reference specifically asked consultants to address the following:

- the assessment, organisation and procurement of planned preventive building maintenance and the establishment of benchmark costs for building maintenance across the sector

- the organisation and procurement of the minor works programme of backlog health and safety related repairs

- the actual and potential uses of facilities management organisations to advise on, organise and deliver general building maintenance and the minor works programme of backlog health and safety related repairs

- the organisation and procurement of major capital works, including the construction of new buildings and the refurbishment of existing premises

- the selection and appointment of consultants to advise on matters relating to estate management and the evaluation of the services provided.

1.2   In addition to the above matters, the guide also includes a separate chapter on the management of a college property portfolio. This chapter considers the role property management can play in helping a college achieve its teaching and business objectives, in addition to more detailed matters such as ethical considerations.

1.3   The guidance has been compiled following both primary and desk-based research including the following:

- detailed surveys and interviews with a sample of colleges

- a review of good practice in the public sector

- a review of good practice in the private sector.

1.4   The findings from the above research activities were validated by seeking feedback from a further sample of colleges.

1.5   The guide is intended to be used as a practical working document whilst also addressing issues that are of strategic importance to colleges. It has been targeted at a broad range of users and aims to provide colleges with sufficient information upon which to base decisions. It also provides a reference for finding further information if required.

1.6   The guide gives generic advice of broad applicability but avoids being prescriptive and advocating solutions which fail to take account of the unique characteristics and circumstances of each college. It is hoped that colleges will wish to use the guide as a framework for the development of more detailed guidance for the day-to-day management of the estate.

2 BACKGROUND TO THE GUIDE

2.1   Following incorporation in April 1993, the control and management of estate matters became the responsibility of individual colleges. In many instances, colleges inherited a major backlog maintenance problem. To alleviate this, the FEFC instigated a condition survey by Hunter & Partners to help identify the extent of the problem and to give an indication of the cost of remedial works across the sector.

2.2   In November 1993, colleges were provided with a document entitled *Guidance on Estate Management* by the FEFC and were requested to provide accommodation strategies by July 1994. The purpose of the accommodation strategy was to review the existing college estate and to evaluate the opportunities and options for rationalisation and/or development to support the strategic goals of the institution. The principal areas of guidance contained within the FEFC publication refer to:

- accommodation strategies

- maintenance investment plans (MIP)

- planned maintenance programmes (PMP)

- space utilisation

- investment appraisal.

2.3   As a consequence of colleges becoming responsible for their own estates, the need for information and advice on good practice has become more important.

2.4   Some of the estate management functions and activities that colleges now need to carry out are outside the traditional core skills of estates-related staff at the date of incorporation. This has led to the need for new appointments, structures and skills to be introduced. In many colleges, estates departments or facilities management departments have been established whilst in others the former arrangements with the local education authorities have been extended, although normally on a more formal contractual basis than before incorporation.

2.5   Estate management practices within the sector vary widely. In some colleges, all aspects of estate management are contracted out, usually with one individual in the management team responsible for estates matters. In others, large estates departments and direct labour teams have been formed which undertake the majority of estates activities in house.

2.6   It is against this background that the good practice guide has been prepared. The good practice guide aims to remove some of the mystique of facilities management (FM) highlighting when it may be advantageous to contract out services and when it is not. It looks at the procurement of major and minor capital works. It considers the assessment, organisation and procurement of planned preventive maintenance (PPM) and, finally, gives guidance on how to procure the services of external consultants.

3 SCOPE OF THE GUIDE

3.1   The good practice guide offers guidance to colleges on the following five key topic areas:

a.   the management of a college portfolio. Chapter 2 addresses the issues of where property fits within the college hierarchy and how it can assist in achieving the institution's strategic objectives and goals;

b.   facilities management. Chapter 3 gives a description of the term, where it may be appropriate for colleges and under what circumstances;

c.   chapter 4 addresses works contracting and planning of major and minor works and discusses in detail the different contract strategies that colleges may enter into. It also covers the selection and evaluation of tenders and risk management;

d.   planned preventive maintenance. Chapter 5 initially addresses the base data that colleges need to gather, then covers the links between MIPs and planned maintenance programmes before discussing organisation and procurement and finally commenting on benchmark costs;

e.   chapter 6 considers procurement and management of consultancy services: the process of selecting, inviting and appointing consultants to provide advice to colleges along with the procedures and processes for monitoring and managing the consultant when appointed.

3.2   There is a need to ensure that, when putting the guide into practice or developing detailed operational guidance, this is done in a manner consistent with any other guidance or instruction prepared by a college such as financial procedures. **In any event, guidance issued by the FEFC is deemed to override any conflicting guidance contained in this document.**

3.3   At the time of compilation of the good practice guide (spring/summer 1995), the recommendations of the Latham report (see further reading list in chapter 4) are still being considered by a number of task forces reporting to a Review Implementation Forum. The Latham report critically addressed current procurement and contractual arrangements and it is likely that, as a result of the report's recommendations, there will be some rationalisation and consolidation of the multitude of procurement and contractual arrangements in operation. Amongst other things, recommendations relate to the role and duties of a project manager, the assessment of tenders and the preparation of a register of consultants for public sector work.

3.4   Colleges will, therefore, need to maintain an awareness of changes in recommended practice that may emerge from the Latham report in particular.

4 HOW TO USE THE GUIDE

4.1   The good practice guide has been prepared in the knowledge that it may be used by different individuals within the college for different purposes. For example, the chapter on procurement of consultants could be used for appointing valuation or rating surveyors, whereas chapter 4 includes guidance on the various contract strategies available to a college intending to procure capital works.

4.2   The guide has, therefore, been prepared as five stand-alone chapters although there are common themes and procedures running through them all. Indeed, there is an element of repetition among the chapters on works contracting and the procurement of consultancy services with the aim of creating 'self-contained' chapters and minimising the need to cross-refer between chapters. This document is not intended to be an all-encompassing guide for every aspect of the estate management function. Instead, the intention has been to pick five priority areas where colleges have indicated that they require particular help and guidance.

4.3   Each chapter starts with a short statement summarising the purpose of the specific guidance and then sets out the key issues to be addressed. Prior to discussing these issues in detail, the guidance contains a 'caution' box which highlights issues where particular care should be taken. References are also provided for the benefit of those seeking further information.

4.4   When reading this guide, users will need to cross-refer as appropriate to other guidance or instruction prepared and issued by the FEFC or the college.

4.5   The appendix to the guide contains a list of addresses of professional institutions, research bodies and other organisations from which further reading material may be sourced.

Chapter 2

MANAGEMENT OF A COLLEGE PROPERTY PORTFOLIO

In this chapter, guidance is given on the management of a college property portfolio in the context of the college's core business.

KEY ISSUES

1   Support to Core Business

2   Management Skills

3   Information

4   Systems and Procedures

5   Ethical Considerations

CAUTION

- The estate can only support the core business in an effective manner if properly resourced

- Continually question the cost and value of information

- Procedures should not be so rigid as to deny innovation.

FURTHER READING

Audit Commission	*Local Authority Property: A Management Handbook*, 1988
DES (DFE)	*Property Information Systems and the Educational Building Stock*, 1986 (A&B Paper No 10)
T. Dixon	*Software Selection for Surveyors*, RICS, 1991
T. Dixon et al	*Microcomputers in Property*, E & F N Spon, 1991
Surrey County Council/Kingston Polytechnic	*The Economic, Efficient and Effective Management of Public Authority Landed Estates*, 1989
The Staff College	*FE: The Built Environment and Incorporation*, 1992
DFEE	*Design Note 31: Educational Planning in North America*, 1992
DFEE	*Design Note 37: Assessing the Capacity of Further Education Buildings*, 1984

DFEE   *Design Note 41: Accommodation for
              Changes in Public Sector Higher Education,*
              1985

DFEE   *Design Note 49: Further Education and
              Sixth Form Colleges – Development
              Strategies for Accommodation,* 1992

DFEE   *Design Note 50: Accommodation for
              Changes in Further Education,* 1994

University of *Managing Operational Property Assets,*
Reading   1989

1 SUPPORT TO CORE BUSINESS

1.1   Property assets, by their nature, tend to be durable and have a relatively long life. As a result of this, deterioration in the structure, fabric or services can often be overlooked and management and maintenance can become reactive rather than proactive.

1.2   Increasingly, however, the direct cost and missed opportunities arising from this reactive approach are being identified and brought to the attention of senior management. Property is being recognised as one of the prime assets of an organisation alongside finance and personnel.

1.3   Active management of the estate can help colleges meet their strategic objectives by:

a.   providing sufficient accommodation that is fit for the purpose. An inadequate amount of accommodation will stifle growth whereas surplus accommodation can be a waste of resources. Colleges must be able to interpret their strategic plan and put in place strategies to achieve the optimum level of accommodation in terms of both quality and amount. Working closely with users, the individual with responsibility for the estate (which, for the purposes of this chapter, is entitled the 'estate manager') must continually reappraise existing accommodation to establish the 'degree of fit' with teaching needs;

b.   optimising running costs. Property-related running costs represent a significant revenue commitment for colleges particularly if accommodation within the portfolio is leased. A skilled estate manager should be able to disaggregate costs, at least to building level, and keep under review:

   i.   rents (where payable)

   ii.   rates

   iii.   utility costs

   iv.   insurances

   v.   direct labour costs

   vi.   other property-related costs related to cleaning, maintenance, energy, security;

c.   realising value. Surplus or under-utilised accommodation can be disposed of and the proceeds re-cycled to facilitate an expansion or move to alternative accommodation elsewhere;

d.   facilitating change. Through the estate manager, the college can effectively cope with inevitable change by, for example, procuring flexible rather than inflexible accommodation, leasing accommodation to meet short-term needs and entering into contracts with other institutions for support services on a risk and cost-sharing basis;

e.   reflecting the desired image. The nature and condition of the college estate is a prime ingredient in creating an overall image of the college in the eyes of its consumers. Students, teachers, visitors and others may see the estate as representative of the quality of the 'business' being conducted within it.

1.4   The next three sections of this chapter deal with three strategic imperatives, namely, management skills, information, and systems/procedures. These must all be in place and to a sufficient extent before property can be proactively managed. If one of the strategic imperatives is absent or deficient in any manner, it is quite possible that value for money will not be obtained nor will the estate truly facilitate the achievement of business objectives.

GUIDANCE SUMMARY

- The proper management of a college property portfolio can help the college meet its strategic objectives.

2 MANAGEMENT SKILLS

2.1   Estate management is, as the term suggests, a management activity. It is therefore concerned with matters such as organisation, resourcing, reporting, monitoring and control. However, these activities should be performed with the benefit of functional expertise and knowledge. The areas of functional expertise commonly listed under the banner of estate management include:

- building fabric and services maintenance

- valuation

- legislation relating to landlord and tenant, health and safety

- procurement of new works/refurbishment

- space utilisation

- premises acquisition and disposal.

2.2   Ideally, the college estate manager should be vested with all the above-mentioned attributes and areas of expertise. In practice, some areas of expertise may only be required on an ad hoc basis. Examples of such ad hoc requirements would be valuation and lease negotiation skills. Meanwhile, there is likely to be a more continuing demand for building maintenance and contract management skills in the college environment. Similarly, the managerial responsibilities of an estate manager must be in place to secure value for money from the estate management function.

2.3   Since colleges have inherited a wide variety of property portfolios and have diverse strategic (and operational) plans, the particular skills and capabilities required to carry out or manage the workload generated by the estate will vary from college to college. A college facing rapid expansion will place different demands on an estates function from that of a college with the same size and type of estate but intending to maintain the status quo.

2.4   As a minimum, colleges require a dedicated resource at senior level capable of proactively managing the estate with functional skills related to the 'baseline' workload relevant to each college.

2.5   An essential requirement of this dedicated resource is that it should be capable of performing the role of the 'informed customer'. The informed customer sits at the interface between the college and, in this instance, the property market. An understanding of the business of the college and the mechanics of the property market is essential if teaching needs are to be effectively translated into demands for property-related works and services. Within chapter 3, there is further discussion about the importance of the informed customer.

2.6   Decisions on how the work should be undertaken are secondary and not dealt with in this chapter. Whether it is performed by an in-house team, or external contractors or a mix of both is a matter to be judged on overall value for money grounds.

2.7   Beyond being able to manage the baseline of work required to be carried out, the estate manager should be capable of identifying the sporadic demands of the college's estate for works and services. That requires an ability to stand back from the routine of operational estate management and take a strategic perspective. Furthermore, the estate manager should know how to deal with strategic matters and be empowered to do so.

2.8   It is suggested that, as a minimum, the estate manager should be competent to perform the following activities:

- advise on strategy to optimise the use of the college's estate

- play a major role in securing strategic objectives

- manage the implementation of major and minor works

- prepare, control and monitor capital and revenue budgets

- provide economic, efficient and effective management of the college's estate including the provision of specialist advice where necessary

- appoint and manage consultants and contractors to assist in the achievement of strategic and operational objectives

- monitor space utilisation and suitability

- develop service standards and quality systems to meet users' requirements

- establish and maintain an appropriate organisational structure.

2.9   Colleges should avoid placing day-to-day responsibility for estate matters in the hands of an individual with a multitude of other responsibilities. The danger of such an arrangement is that reactive management of the estate will result.

2.10   Governors will be aware of the important role property plays in achieving teaching objectives. In the publication entitled *Guide for College Governors* (1994), the FEFC refers to college buildings as a key resource in the provision of education and training. Similarly, those employees directly involved in estate management activities at the strategic and operational level will be aware of the active management it requires.

2.11   Irrespective of the skills and capabilities of the estate manager, effective management of the estate will be difficult to achieve if the appropriate organisational structures, levels of authority and responsibility and reporting procedures are not established. There is no universally-applicable right way to manage a college portfolio in terms of organisational structure. What is clear, however, is that the college's management structure should facilitate the integration of property considerations into the decision-making process.

2.12   This facilitation may be achieved by:

- establishing a regular forum to discuss property matters

- appointing an individual with prime responsibility for property matters to a position sufficiently high in the management hierarchy

- creating an appropriate reporting structure

- ensuring those responsible for delivering property-related services are aware of corporate objectives and the means whereby the estate can be proactively managed to achieve those objectives.

2.13   As a guide to the different organisational structures that can be established and their relative merits, three options are considered below. It is important to emphasise that any decisions on the organisational structure of an estates function must be set in the context of the college's broader policies on such matters as contracting out and the extent to which the college wishes to integrate the delivery of all estate-related services.

2.14   The three options considered are:

option 1   minimal core function. This envisages an individual with responsibility for a wide range of estate-related services procuring such services from an external contractor or contractors. The estate manager may enter into a facilities management agreement with a single party for the provision of maintenance, catering, cleaning and other support services

option 2   multi-disciplinary team. At the other extreme, the estate function is staffed by a team of professionals and non-professionals. Very little work is contracted out. A substantial direct labour force undertakes cleaning, day-to-day maintenance, security and similar tasks as part of an integrated team

option 3   mixed economy. The estate manager has responsibility for a small in-house team, but also enters into and manages contracts with external contractors. Work is allocated to the in-house team or contractors depending on who is best placed, on value for money grounds, to carry out the work or provide the service.

2.15   The reader is referred to chapter 3 which contains sections on the role of the informed customer and the selection and appointment of facilities management contractors together with chapter 5 which includes a commentary on the organisational options for procuring building maintenance works and services. Professional advice should be sought to assist in identifying and evaluating alternative organisational options.

GUIDANCE SUMMARY

- A core set of competencies is required to effectively manage a college property portfolio.

- Property considerations must be integrated with the wider decision-making processes.

- A wide array of organisational options is available; colleges should critically appraise the options to determine which gives the best fit to their circumstances.

3 INFORMATION

3.1   Information is required quite simply to inform decision making. Without adequate information, colleges may make incorrect and badly-timed decisions or perhaps no decision at all.

3.2   All too often, organisations will gather and analyse information because the systems in place enable this to be done. Insufficient thought may be given to the eventual use of the data.

3.3   In order that colleges' property-related information systems can perform the strategic and operational functions required of them, it is recommended that the following issues are addressed:

- what information is needed to facilitate the strategic and operational decision-making process?

- when is the information required?

- what format should it be in?

- who should provide it?

- reappraisal of the cost and value of existing information systems

- identification of essential information gaps

- putting in place systems to fill gaps.

3.4   The college estate manager can provide strategic advice if armed with information including:

- the teaching direction of the college

- the implications this has for (existing and future) accommodation

- capital value of the estate in terms of existing and alternative use

- relative costs of in-house and external works/service provision

- benchmark property performance data

- notional rental values of freehold accommodation.

3.5   Meanwhile, operational estate management will benefit from access to different (but complementary) data sets including:

- property running costs and trends in same

- space utilisation figures

- feedback from users on fitness-for-purpose and quality of works/services provided by the estates function

- building fabric and services condition survey reports

- details of tenancy and other occupancy agreements (whether college is landlord or tenant)

- building floor-plans, site-plans and services layouts.

3.6 The estate manager should be responsible for holding a record of the estate. This may be computerised or manual but, whatever format it is in, the key for success is integration. By catering for a variety of users, a database using common data will foster the concept of property as a corporate asset.

3.7 The prime advantage of a computerised information system is the ability it gives to readily manipulate and cross-refer data from different data sources. Accordingly, the estate manager may be able to compare space utilisation requirements with maintenance and utility costs or perhaps analyse the relationship between projected life-cycle costs of a building and its open market value.

3.8 The need for a co-ordinated property-related information system is particularly important for larger colleges. Here, relevant information could be gathered and held by disparate functions. This will inevitably happen if some work is contracted out.

3.9 Co-ordination can be facilitated by electronic links between functions within a college, and between a college and its consultants or contractors. If an external facilities management contractor is managing the operation of a college's building services with the aid of a computerised building management system, there can be advantages in linking the output from such a system to the contractor's in-house systems. At the commencement of this chapter, several publications are listed which give guidance on the selection and use of software to assist the estate manager.

3.10 Although the use of information technology (IT) is not a pre-requisite for successful information management, it can be useful in the following areas:

- computerised timetabling to improve space utilisation

- computerised maintenance management systems to programme maintenance tasks, schedule the use of resources and optimise the expenditure on planned maintenance

- building management systems to optimise property running costs and to ensure an appropriate working environment for occupiers

- computer-aided design technology to effect rapid changes in building layout and maintain an easy to update database of physical assets.

GUIDANCE SUMMARY

- Ready access to information to support strategic and operational decision-making must be available.

- Computerised information systems can yield benefits where large volumes of data require regular updating.

4 SYSTEMS AND PROCEDURES

4.1 Systems and procedures must be put in place by a college to set a framework around and within which the college estate function should operate.

4.2 Procedures on tendering can promote greater economy while those on performance monitoring can promote improved efficiency. Procedures to be followed in post-project evaluation can aid the measurement of effectiveness. All aspects of value for money can, therefore, be pursued with the aid of appropriate procedures.

4.3 To be effective, procedures must be consistently applied and roles and responsibilities must be clearly established.

4.4 For an estates function to achieve the consistent use of procedures, the most successful way of bringing procedures to the attention of all those affected by them is through the preparation of an 'estate management manual' or similar. This would supplement the good practice guide by giving operational guidance on the detailed implementation of the good practice guide and any college-specific estate policies.

4.5 As procedures will involve the estates function interacting with other college functions, all parties must be made aware of their respective roles and responsibilities. It is evident that a maintenance management system, for example, will operate more effectively with the co-operation of space users before, during and after any necessary works are carried out.

4.6 Procedures based on good practice should be used to avoid colleges being accused of lack of probity in the use of public funds.

4.7 Procedures should be set out in relation to procuring works and professional services which detail the level of delegated authority to the estates function and individual responsibilities within it. These procedures need to be consistent with the college's financial regulations and provide a satisfactory audit trail for authorisation and payment of all contractors' and consultants' claims.

GUIDANCE SUMMARY

- The good practice guide could be supplemented by a detailed estate management manual or similar.

- Estate-related procedures must be consistent with other relevant guidance, procedures and instruction.

5 ETHICAL CONSIDERATIONS

5.1   There is an expectation that organisations engaged in public business will do so within a framework of procedures and controls which will ensure proper conduct. Some elements of these controls are legally required through the instrument and articles of governance. Others will have been adopted by colleges in codes of conduct or purchasing guidelines. At the root of such procedures and controls are the concepts that public money should be spent in such a way as to provide fair and open competition and that people in public positions should not use those positions to gain personal profit. In a report entitled *The Proper Conduct of Public Business* (1994), the government's public accounts committee emphasised the need for relevant organisations to address financial controls, compliance procedures, stewardship of public money and assets and the provision of value for money.

5.2   If they have not already done so, colleges should specifically prepare and promote the use of guidance relating to:

a.   declarations of interest. For example, governors are prohibited from taking or holding any interest in college property without the written approval of the secretary of state for education and employment. Furthermore, any financial and other interests (held by a governor or member of staff) in any matter under discussion by the governing body must be declared and the individual holding that interest must not participate in these discussions. It is expected that colleges will maintain and regularly review a register of financial and other interests;

b.   confidentiality of items of business which the governing body and senior management decide should remain confidential. Such items of business might be the evaluation of tenders although guidance is given elsewhere on feedback that can usefully be given to successful and unsuccessful tenderers following a competition. In general, however, openness of decision-making is to be pursued;

c.   the offer and receipt of gifts and hospitality;

d.   action in the event of improper behaviour. Beyond acting in an ethical manner, colleges must be seen, by those outside as well as those within, to be doing so. This could, for example, result in contractors being struck off the college's approved list;

e.   systems to record and monitor evidence of fraudulent behaviour. This may entail internal auditing of the procurement processes for a sample of projects to complement ongoing systems of data collection and cross-referencing of data sets (for example, consistency between works recorded as completed and approved certificates for payment).

5.3   As a general rule, colleges should take no action that cannot be explained publicly.

GUIDANCE SUMMARY

- Specific guidance should be developed and promoted in connection with ethical considerations.

Chapter 3
FACILITIES MANAGEMENT

● ●

This chapter considers the actual and potential uses of facilities management organisations to advise on, organise and deliver general building maintenance and the minor works programme of backdated health and safety related repairs.

KEY ISSUES

1	What is Facilities Management?
2	The Informed Customer Role
3	Packaging of Services
4	Contract Strategy
5	Selection and Appointment of Contractors
6	Collaboration

CAUTION

- Avoid awarding a packaged facilities management contract to a functional specialist

- Colleges need someone of sufficient skill and authority to effectively manage a facilities management contractor

- A facilities management contractor with its own in-house teams of service providers might not deliver best value for money.

FURTHER READING

A. Park	*Facilities Management; An Explanation*, MacMillan, 1994
CIOB	*CIOB Handbook of Facilities Management*, Longman, 1994
C. Arnold	*Facilities Management Contracts*, Longman, 1994
Oxford Brookes University/ University of Reading	*Property Management Performance Monitoring*, 1993
RICS	*Facilities Management: Today's Challenge, Tomorrow's Profession?*, 1993
Facilities Management Journal	Various articles

1 WHAT IS FACILITIES MANAGEMENT?

1.1   Facilities management (FM) is **not** another phrase for contracting out certain activities nor is it the management of operational activities such as catering, cleaning and building maintenance in isolation.

1.2   It is essentially a management discipline and has been defined as:

'The practice of co-ordinating the physical workplace with the people and work of an organisation.'

(Association of Facilities Managers)

1.3   The implication of the above definition is that true FM is about the following:

- supporting the core business of an organisation

- understanding the impact the workplace can have on people and how they perform in an organisation

- a multi-disciplinary approach to the above.

1.4   All of this suggests that the facilities manager must be a multi-skilled individual capable of turning his or her hand to a wide variety of tasks. The facilities manager must have an in-depth understanding of the core business and the non-core activities that support it so that these can be procured in a way that achieves the best value for money. The facilities manager must be an effective interpreter of business needs. The facilities manager can be an individual employed by the college or an external agent (such as a contractor or consultancy firm).

1.5   It is necessary to determine whether value for money is maximised by providing non-core (support) services in-house or by commissioning them from elsewhere. The typical facilities manager will spend a significant proportion of time managing contracts and, as a consequence, the role has become almost synonymous with the contracting out of services.

1.6   This view of the facilities manager as a manager of contracts is repeating itself in many business sectors as management reorganises to focus on the core business, whether that be manufacturing, banking or the provision of an education service. Additional impetus has been given to this trend in the public sector by the private finance initiative (PFI). One means of transferring risk and thereby achieving a core objective of the PFI is by selective packaging and tendering of services including support services.

1.7   The business support areas that a college facilities manager might have responsibility for include:

- estate management

- security

- cleaning

- transport

- telecommunications/IT

- catering

- design/space planning

- furniture

- estate strategy.

1.8 In many instances, however, there are clear demarcations within the FE sector between the purely premises-related support activities and others.

GUIDANCE SUMMARY

- FM is concerned with the integration of accommodation with people and the business of an organisation.

- Identifying and appraising alternative means of procuring non-core services is a key function of the facilities manager.

2 THE INFORMED CUSTOMER ROLE

2.1   The term 'informed customer' is given to an individual who has the skills and training to act as a knowledgeable interface between the college and a contractor. Whilst the individual is not expected to be an expert in every area of the built environment, his or her knowledge will allow the competent management of relevant college activities.

2.2   Mention has been made of the interpreter role of the facilities manager positioned between business needs (as defined in the strategic plan of a college) and the relevant support services.

2.3   This is a critical characteristic of the facilities manager for without it, the business managers (in the form of the board of governors and senior management teams) may be charting a very different course to that of the facilities manager.

2.4   The facilities manager must control and administer a dialogue and two-way flow of information. On the one hand, business needs must be distilled down into demands for support services which must be commissioned or instructed in a language and framework that will deliver the quality of business support needed. Similarly, the board of governors and/or senior management will need to be kept informed of significant issues that are made known to the college in the form of a technical report by consultants or contractors.

2.5   If the college does not benefit from an individual that can perform the informed customer role (otherwise known as the client's agent), it risks the following:

- misinterpreting the needs of the college for support services

- poor value for money through ineffective contracting and monitoring

- lack of integration in the provision of support services

- not identifying the most appropriate and cost-effective solutions to a problem

- failure to capitalise on the opportunities inherent in the property portfolio.

GUIDANCE SUMMARY

- The facilities manager, whether a college employee or an external consultant, must be able to perform the role of the informed customer.

- Absence of an individual to perform this role can expose the college to significant risks.

3 PACKAGING OF SERVICES

3.1   At the time of writing (November 1995) there is some evidence of colleges creating and sustaining co-ordinated FM functions.

3.2   Despite this trend, few colleges have contracted out packages of support services, preferring instead to manage the delivery of support services in-house. The reasons for this include:

- a reticence within some colleges to contract out

- the failure of FM contractors to convince colleges of the benefits of contracting out

- the clear orientation of some FM contractors towards one particular discipline or another

- the relatively low value of the potential business from smaller colleges.

3.3   In the research which has resulted in this guide, it was noted that reluctance to contract out support services often stemmed from nothing more than a bad experience with a specific contractor. College management should keep an open mind on this issue. It should be recognised that the quality of service delivered can be affected by the inadequacies of a specification and the project management skills employed just as it can be affected by the inadequacies of the consultant or contractor.

3.4   Organisations often hold a belief that support services should not be contracted out because the nature of the business is unique. While it may be true that the core business of an organisation is somewhat unique, services required to support that core business are likely to share common characteristics with support services in other business sectors.

3.5   Colleges should therefore appreciate that, while the core business is radically different from, say, the business of retailing or banking, all require people to perform activities within a built environment.

GUIDANCE SUMMARY

- There is much similarity between the support (or non-core) activities of colleges and organisations in other business sectors.

- Colleges should maintain an open mind on the advantages (and disadvantages) of contracting out support services subject to a detailed appraisal of the options available.

4 CONTRACT STRATEGY

4.1   At one extreme, the contract strategy to be adopted might envisage the procurement and management of all facilities support services being contracted out. At the other end of the spectrum, a college may wish to organise, manage and, indeed, staff all facilities support services using internal resources. More likely, however, is the scenario where some support services are provided by contractors and others by in-house resources.

4.2   There is no model strategy that can be applied by all colleges. Since incorporation, some colleges have taken the opportunity of rationalising the delivery of their support services following a review of contracts entered into by (or with) the local education authority. This has led, in some instances, to the delivery of a higher quality service at reduced cost.

4.3   Whilst some services must be provided by outside contractors, such as inspections of certain items of plant and machinery required to be conducted by competent persons, the choices available to colleges on how other support services are best delivered should be made on overall value for money grounds.

4.4   When considering the options, colleges should ensure that the full cost of in-house services is calculated for comparison purposes. Such a calculation involves an examination of the opportunity cost of all resources deployed to support the support services. When calculating the opportunity cost of using in-house resources, account should be taken of direct staff and administration costs, and accommodation costs including utilities, together with an apportionment of other overheads.

4.5   In addition to cost considerations, the choice of an appropriate contract strategy and therefore the ultimate mix between in-house and contracted-out provision depends on:

- the college's philosophy towards the transfer of risk recognising that risk transfer is typically associated with a cost penalty

- the need for flexibility to adapt to changing service delivery needs

- the college's ability to identify and appraise comparative costs of alternative solutions

- the in-house capabilities within the college to effectively manage the integrated delivery of support services

- constraints imposed by, for example, existing contracts.

4.6   The practicalities of contracting-out mean that a college may lose the services of an established direct labour force unless the successful external contractor takes over responsibility for employment of some or all of these individuals. In due course, when a contract is subsequently re-tendered, there may be less opportunity to effect a continuation of the labour force. Contracting out can, therefore, be associated with a certain amount of instability.

4.7   Where confidential or otherwise important information is handed over, for example, to enable the FM contractor to establish and maintain a property database or building management system, safeguards will need to be built into any contract to guarantee the return of such information in a required format. Where a possibility exists that data will need to be transferred from one FM contractor to another, the smooth transition can be facilitated by incorporating appropriate terms in the FM contract.

4.8   Where the FM contractor is acting as an agent on behalf of the college and separately tenders works and service packages to subcontractors, the college will need to ensure that provision is incorporated in the contract to replace subcontractors if the client can show just cause.

4.9   Professional advice should be obtained to determine which strategy is most appropriate given the particular objectives and relative priorities of each college.

GUIDANCE SUMMARY

- The choice between alternative procurement strategies for support services should be made on value-for-money grounds.

- The full practicalities of contracting out (including the impact on any direct labour force) should be assessed in advance of any decision on procurement strategy.

5 SELECTION AND APPOINTMENT OF CONTRACTORS

5.1   The procedures to be adopted for the selection and appointment of an external FM contractor are essentially the same as those set out elsewhere in this good practice guide for the procurement of consultancy services and contractors (see chapters 4, 5 and 6).

5.2   However, particular attention needs to be paid to the following:

a.   relevant experience. The packaging of services, as mentioned above is a relatively modern phenomenon. Colleges should therefore explore the extent of relevant experience and be prepared to take up references;

b.   FM delivery can be via either a contractor or an agent. Some FM organisations provide the majority of services internally and only subcontract specialist activities, whilst others act as agents managing subcontractors on behalf of the college. Either approach can provide value for money if the procedures and processes are in place to ensure this;

c.   beyond acting as an agent on behalf of the college (if this is to be the prime role), what added value will the FM contractor bring? Colleges should objectively analyse the techniques, technology and management processes that the FM contractor proposes to utilise and question how they will make the college's core business more effective;

d.   understanding of the business (of delivering a learning experience). The FM contractor should understand the motives and methods of working in a college. To be effective, the FM contractor will need to enter into a closer partnership with the client (the college) than is perhaps necessary for a provider of a distinct product or service;

e.   the need for performance specifications concerning the frequency and quality of service. This is particularly important where a contract is to be of more than one year's duration and where there is a danger that the FM contractor's initial enthusiasm and commitment will decline. Declining service can be a problem with term contracts and colleges might consider the inclusion of a clause in contracts for early determination in the event of particularly poor service.

GUIDANCE SUMMARY

- The processes to be followed in the selection and appointment of an external FM contractor reflect those for the procurement of consultants and general contractors.

- Specific considerations apply to the procurement of external FM services.

6 COLLABORATION

6.1   When considering the best way forward for the delivery of support services, the experiences of other educational institutions should be considered. This may require little more than simply discussing problems and possible solutions with counterparts in other colleges. There can also be merit in learning from the experiences of organisations from other business sectors, such as health care, where many parallels can be drawn.

6.2   When procuring works or services from external contractors and consultants, colleges should explore opportunities that may exist to join forces with other educational institutions. The increased purchasing power from such joint ventures could achieve the more economic and efficient delivery of support services. Such an approach could also widen the scope of prospective FM service deliverers by simply putting together a package of greater value to the market.

6.3   To some degree, this type of collaboration exists in that some colleges are continuing to procure services from the local education authority and, by so doing, benefit from the greater purchasing power of the 'partner'. Irrespective of the type of collaborative venture entered into, colleges must be able to demonstrate that the selected procurement route offers best value for money given their particular circumstances.

GUIDANCE SUMMARY

- There is scope within many colleges to package the provision of services and to explore the collaborative procurement of services.

CASE STUDY

College X inherited a significant number of separate FM contracts from the local authority. Management recognised that these contracts were difficult to control, not necessarily cost effective, and that many could be packaged. The college was not in a position to replace contracts with wider packages due to varying end dates. In response to this problem, contracts have been renewed on a short-term basis and plans now exist to undertake a full review when all long-term contracts have come to an end. A full appraisal will be undertaken and specialist consultants will be employed to advise on the best package of FM contracts to meet the college's specific needs.

CASE STUDY

College Y, which had previously contracted with a number of organisations to provide a range of maintenance and related services, evaluated these arrangements and made a conscious decision to move to a true FM arrangement. A contract was established with an external FM contractor on a fixed fee basis covering a range of services, including maintaining plans of the site and buildings, managing major contracts, conducting the annual building conditions survey report, as well as updating the accommodation strategy. Additional services were available on a percentage fee or consultancy basis.

This approach was seen as being the most flexible and cost-effective method of delivering certain estate management activities, where the college contracts directly for a package of services and has preferential access to other services on a contract by contract basis. The college retains an informed customer who regularly monitors the performance of the FM contractor.

CASE STUDY

College Z has consciously adopted the philosophy of FM and is working towards a fully integrated and holistic approach to all its estate management activities. Previously unsatisfactory performance by external contractors (providing individual services such as cleaning) led the college to develop its own in-house capabilities. The college now maintains its own cleaning, grounds maintenance, security and general building maintenance operations. All of these services are delivered to standards laid down in the college's own quality assurance manual which sets out required activities on a weekly, monthly and annual basis. It is understood by the college that the cost and quality of service provision from the in-house team needs to be regularly assessed against that of external providers and the agreed standards in the quality assurance manual will be used as a yardstick. Cleaning will be the first service to be tested at the end of the financial year. The recently computerised building management system already provides for strict energy control and will be developed to manage the planned maintenance programme, replacing the paper system already in use.

Chapter 4
WORKS CONTRACTING

● 31

4

This chapter sets out the organisation and procurement of both the minor works programme of backlog health and safety related repairs and major capital works including the construction of new buildings and the refurbishment of existing premises.

KEY ISSUES

1	Planning the Works
2	Contract Strategy
3	Forms of Contract
4	Selecting Tenderers
5	Inviting Tenders
6	Receipt and Opening of Tenders
7	Tender Evaluation
8	Awarding Contracts and Declining Tenders
9	Recording Recommendations
10	Performance Monitoring
11	Risk Assessment and Management

CAUTION

- Changes in specification can lead to cost escalation

- Early professional advice can prevent later complication

- An inappropriate contract strategy can expose colleges to unnecessary risk.

FURTHER READING

Department of the Environment	*Managing Works Services*, 1993
HMSO	*Constructing the Team (The Latham Report)*, 1994
HMSO	*The Public Works Contracts Regulations*, 1991 (SI 2680)
National Joint Consultative Committee for Building	*Code of Procedure for Two Stage Selective Tendering*, 1994

National Joint Consultative Committee for Building	*Code of Procedure for Single Stage Selective Tendering*, 1994
HM Treasury	*Economic Appraisal in Central Government*, 1992
HM Treasury	*The Economic Appraisal of Property Options: A Manual of Procedures and Techniques*, 1994
HM Treasury	*Central Unit on Procurement Guidance (for example, No 41, Managing Risk and Contingency for Works Projects)*
Further Education Funding Council for Wales	*Financial Management of Building Works*
FEFC	*Purchasing by FEFC Sector Colleges*, 1995
RICS	*Selection and Appointment of the Project Manager*, 1995
FEFC	*Guidance on Estate Management*, 1993

1 PLANNING THE WORKS

1.1 At various points throughout this chapter, reference is made to major capital projects. The guidance is, however, applicable to all projects involving the commissioning of works contractors directly or through an intermediary (for example, a project manager).

1.2 A contract is only the outcome of a chosen strategy for the project in question. Rigorous analysis of alternative courses of action and appraisal of particular options may be needed before a decision to set up and let a contract can be made.

1.3 The level of planning required for works contracts will vary with the quality, complexity and scale of a project. In addition each college will have, as part of its financial regulations, procedures and processes which will need to be followed when considering appointing contractors, professionals or undertaking works.

What planning needs to be carried out?

Are there any specific techniques which should be adopted?

Purpose of Planning

1.4 Planning is one of the most fundamental tools used in the management of businesses. The purpose of plans is not to define exactly what will occur, but to set out the parameters of what is likely to occur so that logical decisions about future events can be taken. For colleges, planning must occur at the strategic level in the first instance to set the context for the preparation of building-related projects.

Initial Feasibility

1.5 A common cause for complaint in the construction sector is that clients do not know what it is they want at the outset of a project. This ultimately manifests itself in the design and construction of a building that does not match their needs. There is much to be said for involving users at an early stage in the planning process and involvement could extend to participating in the preparation of specifications. For colleges, users could include teaching staff and student representatives.

1.6 If an inadequate brief is presented to a design team and/or a contractor it can lead to subsequent changes being necessary. This can lead to major cost and time overruns and performance that is below expectations. Inadequate planning and monitoring of a project at inception and during the works can be the principal cause of such problems.

1.7 Major capital projects are not quick fixes, nor do they resolve problems overnight. Quick decisions and hurried processes are therefore to be avoided.

1.8 The starting-point in planning a project is to assess whether the perceived need is an actual need or whether other options or opportunities exist that may provide better value for money. In many instances this simple process is ignored in the haste to construct, refurbish or buy a building to resolve an immediate problem. Other less capital-intensive options, such as sharing premises, renting space and using existing buildings more effectively, need to be considered.

1.9   In many colleges, this assessment (option appraisal) exercise can be carried out internally although for large or complex capital projects, independent advice should be considered.

1.10   This option appraisal exercise does, however, need to be seen as independent from the eventual capital project. For example, it would be inappropriate to appoint an adviser to help a college prepare a project viability option if the same adviser is to be used as the project manager should the project proceed.

1.11   The purpose of the planning stage is primarily to determine the following:

- what are the college's strategic objectives as far as is relevant to the project being considered?

- does the accommodation strategy facilitate the achievement of these strategic objectives?

- is this project consistent with the accommodation strategy?

- what alternative options have been considered?

- what are the costs, benefits and uncertainties of each option?

- what approvals are required — internal and external?

- is independent advice necessary?

- who within the college will be responsible for the project?

1.12   Having decided to proceed with a project, the principal issue to be decided is how to procure the works. In deciding on the appropriate contract strategy, the college will need to be aware of the interrelationship of three key variables: *time, cost and quality.*

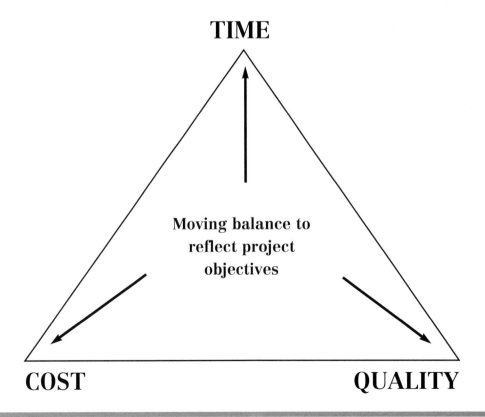

1.13   In a well-managed project, the three objectives highlighted in the diagram on the previous page will be continually managed and the inevitable tensions kept under control. If one objective becomes dominant, it will impact on the others. If, for example, a college's need was to procure a building as fast as possible, it may have to accept that this could impact on the cost of the building. Alternatively, if the performance of the building needs to be to a very high standard, then this could impact on the time needed to build the project.

Planning Works Contracts

1.14   All works contracts require planning. The extent to which colleges should undertake this work internally depends on the competence and availability of the existing staff. If this work is to be undertaken by external professionals, they should be under the control and guidance of a member of the college's staff. Generally, however, the larger and more complex a works contract, the more likely it is that the college should give consideration to the appointment of an external project manager to act as the college's client representative. Parallels are drawn here with the role of the facilities manager as the informed customer.

1.15   An external project manager will act as the clients' representative and will be responsible for controlling the works contract and the professional team. Appointing a project manager will not, however, completely remove the need for the involvement of college staff. A specific individual should be responsible for the college's day-to-day input to the project and should in essence become the client. This individual will need to be given a degree of delegated authority to make decisions about the project. If well planned contracts have been placed following an assessment of the levels of the likely risks, further significant changes during the contract period are less likely to be required. Any major decision or change should be referred to the level of college management which has the authority to commit further funds or authorise significant changes.

1.16   Managing major works contracts can be very time consuming and require a high level of technical competence. Colleges, whilst still needing to exercise control, should not undertake this role in house unless they have the skills and can commit the resources. Typical issues that need to be addressed and determined before works contracts can be let include:

- controlling a project from start to finish

- defining the brief

- viability studies

- project planning

- appointing a professional team

- agreeing specifications and contract terms

- appointing a contractor

- organising when works should be carried out

- controlling costs

- ensuring different works follow logically from one to another

- checking that payments are made at appropriate times

- supervising works and ensuring they are completed on time, within budget and to an acceptable quality.

Approaches Adopted in Planning Works Contracts

1.17   One of the most straightforward and readily-used methods of planning works contracts is through the use of project bar charts.   These can be used for any project large or small and can be made as simple or complex as the project requires.

1.18   The main advantage of bar charts (see below and overleaf) is their simplicity and flexibility. Each activity involved in a project can be plotted against a timescale with the sequence of activities built up to determine the project duration.

Activities	Weeks															
	1	2	3	4	5	6	7	8	9	10	11	12	13	14	15	16
Agree project brief	▓	▓														
Invite tenders			▓	▓	▓	▓										
Interview						▓										
Commission work							▓									
Phase 1								▓	▓	▓						
Phase 2											▓	▓	▓			
Phase 3														▓	▓	
Final completion																▓

A TYPICAL CONSTRUCTION PROJECT PLANNING BAR CHART

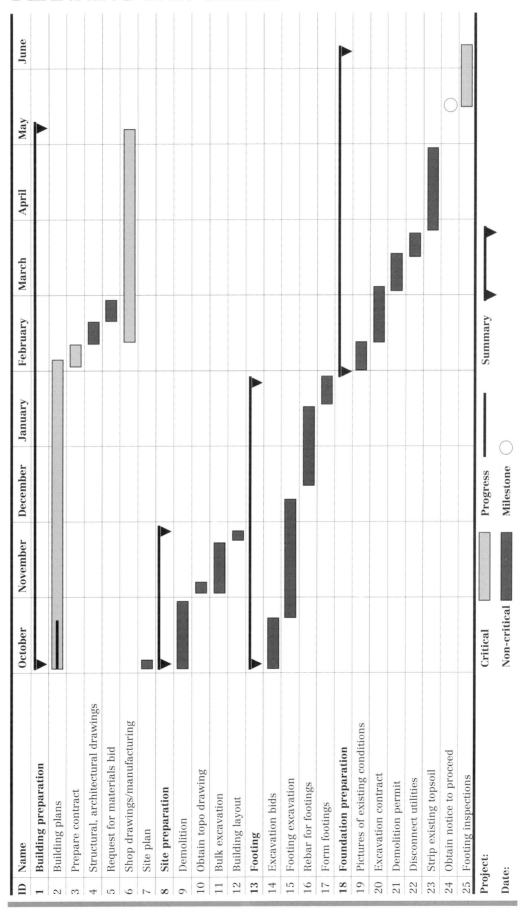

ID	Name	October	November	December	January	February	March	April	May	June
1	**Building preparation**									
2	Building plans									
3	Prepare contract									
4	Structural, architectural drawings									
5	Request for materials bid									
6	Shop drawings/manufacturing									
7	Site plan									
8	**Site preparation**									
9	Demolition									
10	Obtain topo drawing									
11	Bulk excavation									
12	Building layout									
13	**Footing**									
14	Excavation bids									
15	Footing excavation									
16	Rebar for footings									
17	Form footings									
18	**Foundation preparation**									
19	Pictures of existing conditions									
20	Excavation contract									
21	Demolition permit									
22	Disconnect utilities									
23	Strip existing topsoil									
24	Obtain notice to proceed									
25	Footing inspections									

Critical   Non-critical   Progress   Milestone   Summary

Project:

Date:

CASE STUDY

College X recognised that the large quantity of remedial work required to be carried out on the estate would cause substantial disruption to the use of various buildings. The architect appointed to manage the works suggested a comprehensive contract planning process whereby both essential maintenance and upgrading work would be carried out at the same time in order to minimise the period of time each part of the building was out of commission. By using a series of bar charts, the college and its consultant were able to arrange contracts in a logical sequential order. This avoided duplication of work (such as removal of suspended ceilings and electrical wiring) and enabled a much higher standard of improvement to be attained in a similar length of time to that required for the remedial works alone.

1.19 Where bar charts are inappropriate due to the complexity or uncertainty of the project, network planning can be an appropriate alternative project planning technique. This attempts to answer the 'what if?' questions. The output from a network planning exercise is shown opposite. The approach has five principal stages as set out below:

- agree activities

- determine logical relationships

- assess duration of activities

- determine critical path

- optimise plan.

1.20 The starting-point is to set out, in a similar form to the bar chart on page 37, the key activities that are to be undertaken.

1.21 The next stage assesses what activities must be completed before the next activity is started. In the bar chart, the activity 'Agree Project Brief' may have included an estimation of the cost of works, a survey of what is required, or authorisation procedures to go to tender.

1.22 An allocation of the resources and an estimation of the duration of each activity is then required. Times are allocated to activities with each estimate being progressively totalled. The earliest time any activity can start is controlled by the latest finish time of any logically preceding activity. Once all the activities have been determined, the times are added together to give an estimation of the duration of the project. This process is repeated but working from the end of the project to the beginning to determine the latest time an activity must start in order to meet the end date.

1.23 The difference between the earliest start and latest start gives the latitude for slippage. The critical path is the string of individual activities providing the minimum duration of the project within defined constraints.

1.24 The final stage is resource levelling. This calculates the resource requirements for each activity showing up the peaks and troughs. By analysing the network and using the earliest and latest start times, a more even spread of resources can be allocated to a project. The simplified example on the facing page shows six stages of a contract requiring work of electricians. Carried out sequentially, the contract takes six weeks with between 3 and 8 electricians employed at any one time. As the last 3 stages, D, E and F are not dependent on completion of the first 3 stages, A, B and C, resource levelling can be used to reduce the contract time to 3 weeks with between 11 and 12 electricians employed per week. Such an approach will not only shorten the duration of a works contract but reduce cost by minimising the contractor's staff movements and set-up times. Computer software is available to assist the project manager prepare critical path or network diagrams and arrive at the optimal scheduling of resources.

EXAMPLE OF RESOURCE LEVELLING

Project stages D, E and F can be carried out independently of A, B and C. They are therefore scheduled in such a way as to minimise fluctuations in the number of electricians required on the project. In this simplified case, stage E would be carried out at the same time as stage A, D at the same time as B and so on, keeping the combined level of electricians required as smooth as possible.

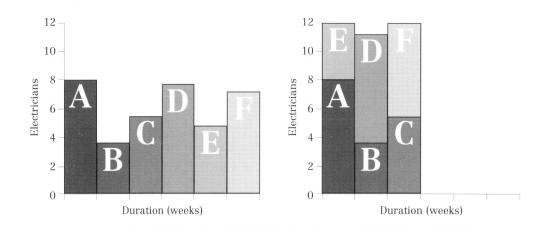

1.25   Either of these methods (bar charts or network diagrams) can be used to plan works contracts. The actual method of planning is of less importance than the process of trying to foresee in advance of a project what issues, resources, timing and cost will be needed to achieve the objectives. Planning is a powerful management tool and one that colleges should devote sufficient time and resources to if value for money is to be rigorously pursued.

GUIDANCE SUMMARY

- Allow sufficient time for the planning process.

- Seek early professional advice where appropriate.

- Define clearly project objectives – make them measurable.

- Consider and appraise a range of options and select the most appropriate to the college's circumstances.

- Ensure necessary approvals, internal and external, are sought.

- Use a recognised technique for planning and monitoring a project.

- Understand the balance between time, cost and quality.

- Appoint a member of college staff as the key contact point with the contractor.

STEPS FOR CONSIDERING AND SELECTING A CONTRACT STRATEGY

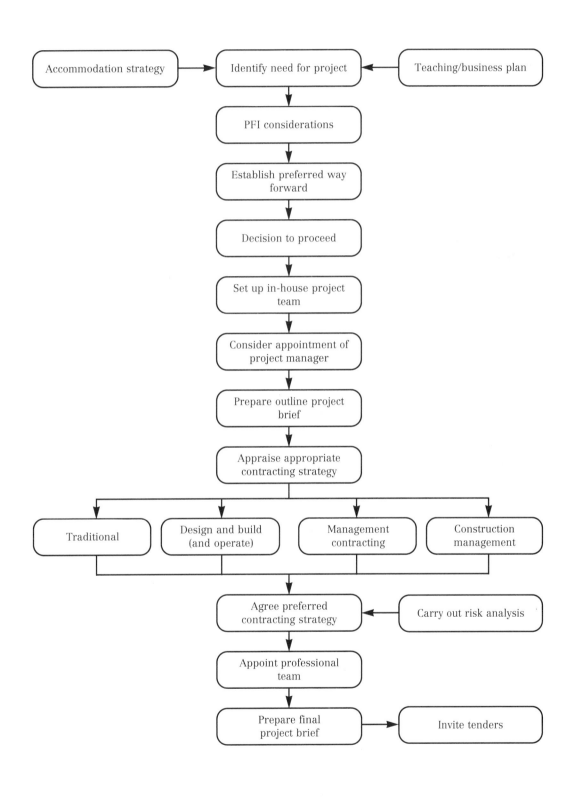

2   CONTRACT STRATEGY

2.1   This section considers the different forms of contract strategy that are available to colleges when undertaking works projects. It compares the most common forms and gives advice on which is most appropriate under different circumstances.

What forms of contract strategy are there?

Which is the most appropriate?

Under which circumstances?

2.2   The type of contract strategy chosen for a building project is a critical decision for colleges. The chosen strategy will influence the allocation of risk, the project management requirements, the design strategy and the employment of consultants and contractors. It also has a major impact on timescale and, ultimately, the cost of a project.

2.3   Contributing parties to a contract should be encouraged to work together and a successful strategy should result in a completed building which achieves all the college's objectives. The steps a college should follow in selecting a contract strategy are summarised in the table overleaf and are discussed below.

Project Management

2.4   In many major building projects, colleges may wish to appoint a project manager to act on their behalf as an informed customer. The role of a project manager can vary considerably on the basis of the project to be undertaken and with the contract strategy selected. In general, however, a project manager would normally have responsibility for overall planning, control and co-ordination and ensuring the project is completed on time, within cost and to an acceptable quality.

Forms of Contract Strategy

2.5   The main types of contract strategy are as follows:

- Traditional

- Management Contracting

- Design and Manage

- Construction Management

- Design and Build

- Design, Build and Operate.

Traditional

2.6   In this form of contract strategy, the college would engage a professional team to prepare designs and tender documentation for the works. These would be sent out to contractors to bid for the work.   A main contractor would be appointed to undertake the works with subcontractors working directly for the main contractor. On this basis, the college maintains contractual control over both the design team and the contractor.

While this gives a college maximum control over a project, it also gives it considerable risk in terms of the responsibility of the design team and the contractor. The contractor is only assuming responsibility and risk for the building works.

2.7   This form of contract strategy is well tried and tested, although it can be a relatively slow means of procurement, as sufficient time has to be allocated for the design process. A traditional procurement strategy may not always guarantee 'buildability' since the contractor may not be brought into the design process and is often engaged to build to a design prepared exclusively by another party.

TRADITIONAL STRATEGY

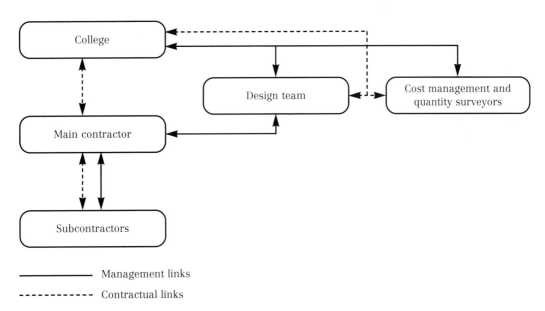

—————— Management links

- - - - - - - - - Contractual links

Source: Adapted from CUP Guidance Note 36 'Contract Strategy Selection for Major Projects', June 1992

Management Contracting

2.8   Management contracting is similar to construction management with the exception that a management contractor is appointed by the college to take responsibility for the contract. In this instance, the individual trade contracts are with the management contractor, not the college. The management contractor will be paid a fee, usually on a percentage basis, and he takes responsibility for the construction work. If a fixed fee is agreed, there is usually some provision for adjusting the actual cost if it varies more than a specified amount from the target cost. The college maintains responsibility and control of the design team. The management contractor does not carry out the work directly, but contracts with individual contractors for work packages. The benefit of a management contract is that not all design works need to be completed before the contract starts which can save time (fast track). It also transfers some of the risk away from the college.

2.9   The disadvantages include uncertainty over the final price as this cannot be guaranteed until the last work package is let. This can, in part, be overcome by agreeing in advance with the contractor a cost plan for the packages. The design of the packages must then come within the pre-determined plan. If not, then the package should be redesigned. There is also no contractual relationship between the college and the trade contractors.

2.10   Under this form of contract, colleges are directly responsible for the main contract through their appointed construction manager. Although this brings with it the ability to be actively involved in the project, it also adds considerable responsibilities, and the college must ensure that its project management team have the technical and commercial skills necessary to undertake the project.

2.11   This contract form is most useful for large and complex contracts where co-ordination of specialists and early completion are vital. As most colleges have time to prepare a considered brief and most college projects are not complex, management contracting is unlikely to be extensively used in the further education sector.

MANAGEMENT CONTRACTING

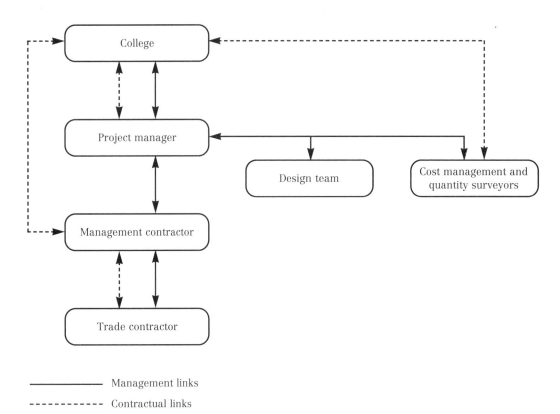

Management links

- - - - - - - - - - - Contractual links

Source: Adapted from CUP Guidance Note 36 'Contract Strategy Selection for Major Projects', June 1992

Design and Manage

2.12   This is very similar to management contracting, with the contractor also being responsible either for the detailed design or for managing the detailed design process. The design and manage contractor is paid a fee to manage and assume responsibility not only for the trade contractors but also for the design team. This has the advantage that the college has to deal with only one firm and the contractor is responsible for integrating design and construction. The principal disadvantages are that the college loses direct control and has no contractual relationship with the design team and trade contractors and price certainty is not achieved until the last work package has been let.

Construction Management

2.13 In this form of contract strategy, no single contractor is appointed and responsibility for design of the project remains with the college through the design team. A construction manager is appointed and has responsibility for controlling and co-ordinating the design and construction of the works. Whilst the college would separately appoint a full design team, the construction manager arranges for the various elements of the construction (works packages) to be tendered to individual contractors. The control and co-ordination of these contractors lies with the construction manager although the individual contractual agreements are with the college.

CONSTRUCTION MANAGEMENT

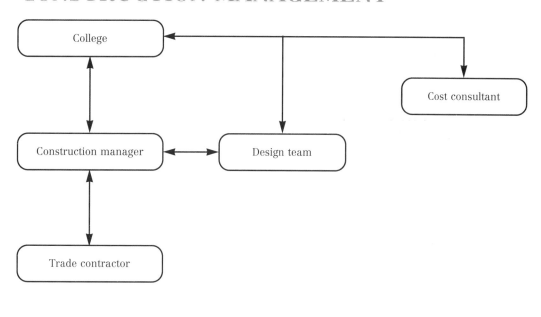

—————— Management links

Contractual links are all
directly with college and
are therefore not shown

Source: Adapted from CUP Guidance Note 36 'Contract Strategy Selection for Major Projects', June 1992

2.14 The advantage of this strategy is that it can allow works to progress quickly, for example, foundation work packages can be awarded before detailed design is completed. It also has the advantage that the construction manager is employed by the college and therefore looks after the college's interests as opposed to a main contractor who may be more interested in making a profit for his company. The disadvantages of this strategy are that an accurate final cost cannot be determined until the last work package has been let, the college takes all of the risk and there is no guaranteed completion date.

Design and Build

2.15 The contractor provides the design and constructs the building for an agreed lump sum. The risk and responsibility for the project are, therefore, transferred to the contractor. The advantage of this form of contract can be speed and cost certainty. Full design does not need to be complete before work starts and certainty of cost is obtained before construction commences. In addition, the college has only to deal with one contractor.

2.16 Most college projects are reasonably simple and suit a design and build approach. The majority of college capital projects have proceeded on this basis even though some of them have required a certain element of pre-contract design. Providing the college draws up precise performance specifications and employers' requirements, design and build gives cost certainty and can be a less expensive method of procurement than a traditional form of contract.

DESIGN AND BUILD

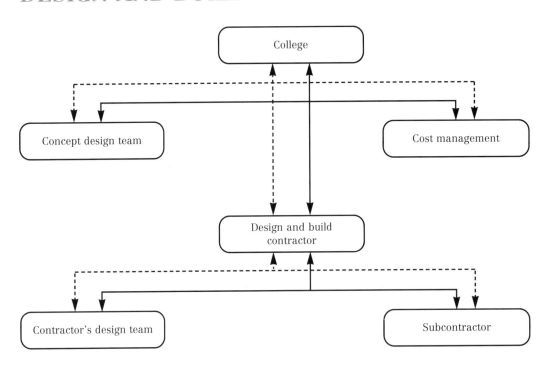

Source: Adapted from CUP Guidance Note 36 'Contract Strategy Selection for Major Projects', June 1992

2.17 Unless the college has sufficient in-house skills, it will need to obtain and pay for professional advice in order to draw up performance specifications and an employer's requirements document. Given that the contractor's design fees will be hidden in the lump sum price, there are effectively two sets of professional fees which the college needs to bear in mind as a price to pay for cost certainty.

2.18 Where a design and build contractor is engaged to complete the preliminary designs of another architect or professional team, the contract strategy is more accurately termed 'Design, Develop and Construct'. This strategy ensures that the college has an important early input to the overall design process.

Design, Build and Operate

2.19 The introduction of the private finance initiative (PFI) in the chancellor's autumn statement of 1992 has increased the use of design, build and operate (DBO) as a procurement route. The design and build element remains as described in the last section with the addition being the responsibility to operate or manage a facility. There are many examples to be found of 'serviced' offices whereby the developer will make accommodation available in return for a payment in respect of rent, rates, utilities, maintenance and so on.

2.20 The use of DBO contracts in the education sector has been very limited, if used at all. The government's active promotion of the PFI could, however, change this significantly.

2.21 A variant of DBO envisages the developer funding the project. In addition to student accommodation provision, where private finance has already been used, there are opportunities to lever in private finance and management expertise when procuring leisure and catering facilities.

2.22 Whenever colleges elect to pursue a DBO/PFI strategy, management must be satisfied that the benefits to be gained by levering in private sector capital and management expertise exceed the additional costs that may be incurred.

Selecting the Most Appropriate Contract Strategy

2.23 The ultimate responsibility for deciding on the contract strategy lies with the college. The choice should, however, be made after careful consideration of the advantages and disadvantages of each approach. Where external advice has been commissioned, a consultant's recommendations should be borne in mind.

2.24 In deciding which approach to adopt, the college needs to consider which strategy best meets the objectives and requirements of the specific project.

2.25 One approach to selecting the appropriate contract strategy is to define a series of criteria and to weight and score each option against these. Weighting the objectives will allow the relative importance of each criteria to the college to be taken into account. The strategy with the highest weighted score is likely to be the most appropriate for the college. An example of the basis of selecting a contract strategy is highlighted on page 53.

2.26 In this hypothetical example, a design and build strategy best meets the college's requirement. This example could represent a college with limited internal resources to co-ordinate or control a design team and a fixed budget, which wants a straightforward

Criteria	Requirement	Weighting	Traditional	Design & Build	Management Contracting	Construction Management
Cost	Cost overrun must be avoided – budget cannot be exceeded	4	8(32)	10(40)	2(8)	2(8)
Professional responsibility	Do not have in-house expertise; want this covered by the contract	2	2(4)	10(20)	2(4)	2(4)
Variations	Unlikely to be changes as project progresses	2	3(6)	8(16)	7(14)	7(14)
Risk avoidance	Pass risk to contractor as far as possible	4	5(20)	10(40)	5(20)	3(12)
Total			**18(62)**	**38(116)**	**16(46)**	**14(38)**

Note: *Weighting: 1–5 with 5 critical to procurement*
Scoring: 1–10 with 10 fully achieving criteria
Weighted scores in brackets

building completed at minimum risk. As long as the specification produced is very clear and there are no variations, the strategy should be successful.

2.27 In summary, there is a variety of different contract strategies available for colleges to use to procure a building. The choice of which to adopt depends to a great extent on the type of project being considered, the level of in-house expertise and the nature by which control of the project and risk is allocated. A summary of the advantages and disadvantages of alternative contract strategies is given overleaf.

2.28 In general, for large complex projects colleges should seek external professional advice on the choice of contract strategy, and on page 52, we have also set out a summary table, adapted from Sir Michael Latham *Constructing the Team*, July 1994. This guidance should not, however, be considered as cast in stone, but as giving degrees of appropriateness for each strategy. For example, a traditional contract strategy can be used to procure complex buildings although construction management or management contracting is generally regarded as more appropriate.

GUIDANCE SUMMARY

- Clear objectives need to be established before deciding on a contract strategy.

- Different contract strategies are appropriate for different projects.

- Colleges may wish to appoint a project manager to assist in deciding on a contract strategy.

- External advice may be required to assist the college in choosing a contractor and defining his role in relation to the overall management of the project.

- The professional team should be appointed once the contract strategy is decided.

- The various contract strategies allocate the level of control and risk between the college and the contractor in differing ways.

CONTRACT STRATEGIES – ADVANTAGES AND DISADVANTAGES

4

TRADITIONAL

Advantages	Disadvantages
• Price certainty	• Full design required before tendering – can be time-consuming
• Control over quality of design and construction	• College needs to administer consultants and/or project manager
• Contractual relationship with design team	• Information delays – drawing etc, can lead to claims from contractor
• Recovery of costs from contractor for failure to meet contractual obligations	• No contractor input to design
	• Design risk remains with college

CONSTRUCTION MANAGEMENT

Advantages	Disadvantages
• Can speed up construction time	• Danger of delays/disruption caused by an individual trade contractor
• Can be applied to complex buildings	• College needs skilled resources for administering contracts
• Direct control of design team maintained	• Construction manager assumes no risk
• Poor contractors can be removed more easily	• Price certainly not achieved until all work packages let
• Construction manager works for college – their objectives overlap	
• College has direct contract with trade contractors – can result in lower prices	
• Dispute can usually be resolved more easily without a main contractor	

MANAGEMENT CONTRACTING

Advantages	Disadvantages
• Managing contractor assumes some risk for other contractors	• Responsibility for paying subcontractors with management contractor
• Overlapping activities allow for fast completion	• College has no contract with trade contractors
• Changes can be incorporated on unlet packages	• College needs to have resources to administer design team and management contractor
• Can be used on complex building	• Price cannot be guaranteed until last work package let
• Direct control over design team maintained	

DESIGN AND BUILD

Advantages	Disadvantages
• Contractor responsible for design and construction	• Loss of design control
• College deals with only one firm	• College has no contractual relationships with design or trade contractors
• Overlapping activities allow for fast completion	• Changes to specification can be costly
• Can be applied to complex building	
• No claims for late information	

CASE STUDY

The principle of the design and build procurement strategy is equally applicable to the procurement of minor works as it is to the procurement of new buildings and other large-sized projects. College X decided that it needed to install a modern fire alarm throughout the main campus. A relatively loose brief was prepared and submitted to four specialist contractors for tendering purposes. A variety of approaches were proposed, all of which met the range of objectives set out in the brief to a greater or lesser degree. It was felt by the college that this approach fostered innovation within a framework of objectives that included a cost constraint.

CASE STUDY

Very often, bringing a fresh mind to bear upon a problem can provide rewarding results. When faced with the need to re-organise and redevelop its accommodation College Y approached several contractors for proposals in accordance with the college's own outline plans. An external consultant was subsequently employed to carry out a value management study and was capable of identifying a significantly different preferred solution to the teaching needs of the college.

Project objectives	Appropriateness of contract strategy in meeting project objectives					
Parameter	Objectives	Traditional	Construction management	Management contracting	Design & manage	Design & build
Timing	Early completion	✗	✓	✓	✓	✓
Cost	Price certainty before construction starts	✓	✗	✗	✗	✓
Quality	Prestige level in design and construction	✓	✓	✓	✗	✓✗
Variations	Avoid prohibitive costs of change	✓	✓	✓	✓	✗
Complexity	Technically advanced or highly complex building	✗	✓	✓	✗	✗
Responsibility	Single contractual link for project execution	✗	✗	✗	✓	✓
Professional responsibility	Need for design team to report to sponsor	✓	✓	✓	✗	✗
Risk avoidance	Desire to transfer complete risk	✗	✗	✗	✗	✓
Damage recovery	Ability to recover costs direct from the contractor	✓	✗	✓	✓	✓
Buildability	Contractor input to economic construction to benefit the department	✓	✓	✓	✓	✗

✓ appropriate
✗ not appropriate

Note: This table is for guidance only. Generally the appropriateness of the contract strategy is not as clear cut as indicated.

Source: Adapted from Sir Michael Latham 'Constructing the team', July 1994

3 FORMS OF CONTRACT

3.1   There are many forms of contract available for use when procuring minor and major capital works. In this section, the most common forms of contract suitable for both new build and alteration works are discussed. Given the variety of standard forms of contract available, colleges should seek professional advice to help determine which is most appropriate for the circumstances.

a.   Joint Contracts Tribunal (JCT) 80 With Quantities

The Joint Contracts Tribunal (JCT) is responsible for producing some of the more commonly used standard forms of contract. 'JCT With Quantities' is suitable for medium to large-sized works. It is also suited to complex projects where the design (to be carried out by the college's own consultants) is sufficiently well advanced at tender stage so that meaningful bills of quantities may be produced. Although this standard form of contract is rather complex in places, this has not prevented it from being widely used and understood by consultants and contractors. A significant volume of case law, following the use of this form of contract for project procurement, has helped in the interpretation of many of the form's clauses.

b.   JCT 80 Without Quantities

This form of contract is suitable for medium-sized projects where the design is well advanced, if not complete, at tender stage with the contract being based on a specification and drawings. The absence of a bill of quantities means that post-contract financial control is made more difficult. Since this form of contract necessitates higher tendering costs (coupled with the contractor's increased risk inherent in this type of contract), it will typically result in higher tenders than with contracts where bills of quantities form a component part.

c.   JCT Intermediate Form of Contract (IFC 84)

Suitable for small to medium-sized projects where the comprehensive provisions of 'JCT 80' are felt unnecessary, but where the provisions of the 'JCT Agreement for Minor Building Works' are considered insufficient. Complexity rather than size of contract should, however, be the principal determinant of the type of contract to use. 'IFC 84' could, therefore, be a suitable form of contract for a multi-million pound project for a college which is of a relatively simple and straightforward nature and where the design of a project needs to be well advanced at tender stage.

d.   JCT Agreement for Minor Building Works (MW 80)

'MW 80' is suitable for small and simple projects. It creates a lump-sum contract based on a specification and drawings. The design must be well advanced at tender stage.

e.   JCT Management Contract (MC 87)

This form of contract is suitable where the contractor is engaged to perform a management role on behalf of the college with the work being carried out by works contractors who are employed by the main contractor. It is not unusual for the main contractor and the client to jointly discuss and agree the nature and identity of the works contractors. This form of contract is generally considered suitable for large and complex schemes and can be particularly suitable where an early start on site must be made with the detailed design being carried out by the (college's) design team concurrent with a start on site.

By effectively making the contractor a member of the college's project team, the contract is non-adversarial. The contractor's liability to the college under 'MC 87' for works contractors would be limited to that for which the contractor is in turn able to obtain by way of redress from the works contractors.

f. JCT with Contractor's Design (CD 81)

This is essentially the JCT's version of a design and build contract whereby the contractor is responsible for the design of the works. It provides for a single point of responsibility in the event of any design defects and also cost certainty in that only changes in the college's requirements would entitle the contractor to additional monies. It is suitable for projects of all sizes but perhaps less suited to projects where aesthetics or innovation are being sought or where quality is a major criterion. It is not, however, suitable for projects where the college's requirements at tender stage are difficult to define. This form of contract can heavily penalise clients who insist on post-tender changes to requirements.

g. British Property Federation (BPF)

The BPF form of contract is not very widely used although much of its contents are replicated in the 'JCT with Contractor's Design' form of contract. Furthermore, the general approach of the BPF form of contract is also followed by the NEC (see below).

h. New Engineering Contract (NEC)

This is a very recent innovation and purports to be suitable for civil and engineering works and mechanical and electrical installations with or without the contractor having any design responsibility. By reason of its broad suitability, the compilation of the contract documentation may be more complicated than would be the case with other standard forms of building contract. The NEC, which was subject to widespread consultation and discussion throughout its development period, has been commended in the Latham Report (1994) and noted as incorporating many elements of contracting best practice. It is, however, too early to comment on the practical costs and benefits of this form of contract given its novelty.

i. GC/Works/1

A new version of the GC Works family of contracts has recently been produced. While former versions of the contract were primarily aimed at government bodies, the new version is of much broader application. The terms of this form of contract are more favourable to the employer and overcome some of the shortcomings of JCT 80. In particular, a contractor can obtain extensions of time under JCT 80 for the failure of a subcontractor to perform whereas the main contractor remains fully responsible for the performance of any subcontractors if a GC Works form of contract is used. As such, an extension of time can be more difficult to argue. Colleges should, however, be aware that the extent to which the form of contract protects the employer's interests may be reflected in higher tender prices. A further disadvantage is that there is less case law than with JCT to help users in the interpretation of the terms of the contract.

In general, the GC Works form of contract should be used in circumstances that would also suggest the use of JCT 80 With Quantities.

Control of Contracts

3.2   In this section, we briefly discuss some issues associated with the control and administration of contracts.

a.   Novation of Consultant Team

This refers to a situation whereby the consultant team appointed by the college is re-appointed by a contractor. Upon the signing of a novation agreement, the contractor takes on all of the rights and liabilities of the college in respect of matters occurring both before and after the date of novation.

This strategy can be of advantage to the college where there is merit in achieving the continuity of having certain members of the design team involved throughout the project.

b.   Liquidated Damages for Non-completion

Most standard terms of contracts contain clauses enabling the contracting parties to agree in advance the damages to be paid by the contractor to the employer (the college) in the event of the contractor failing to complete on time. The courts typically uphold liquidated and ascertained damages and welcome them as a sensible alternative to litigation. However, there must be a genuine estimate of the employer's likely losses as opposed to simply a penalty payment. Loss to a college might relate to the inability to accept students because the required teaching accommodation is not available.

In the event of a change to the scope and duration of the contracted work brought about by the client or arising from an event outside the control of the contractor it may be necessary to determine a revised completion date for the contract. Any such revision would need to be founded on the certification of an appropriate validated extension of time based on contractor's claims. In such cases, this may result in a claim for loss and/or expense by the contractor.

c.   Collateral Warranties

Collateral warranties have come about as a result of the concern of tenants, employers and funding institutions about recent developments in the law of negligence depriving the aforementioned of a cause of action against contractors and consultants responsible for defective design and/or construction. A collateral warranty (or more correctly, a collateral contract) is an agreement which subsists alongside another contract and which is related to that other contract. In essence, it binds two parties who would otherwise not have had any contractual relationship, but who are involved in the same project. A funding institution backing a new college development may, therefore, require a warranty from the professional team and main contractor so that, in the event of the developer going into liquidation, the college can require the other parties to complete the project and retain recourse to them for latent defects.

d.   Treatment of Variations to a Contract

Where standard forms of contracts are used, great care must be exercised where variations are made since a minor amendment to one clause may affect many other clauses disproportionately. Legal advice should be sought when a college intends to seek a variation to standard contract terms.

e. Claims Against Colleges

Under standard forms of contract, terms of redress are available to both the employer and the contractor. These terms are detailed within the contract, the full implications of which should be understood before signing any contract. Legitimate claims against a college may be made where, for example, the specification is amended mid-way through a project.

f. The Construction, Design and Management Regulations 1994 (CDM Regulations)

The CDM Regulations, which came into force on 31 March 1995, are to be introduced into the regulatory framework created by the Health & Safety at Work Act 1974. Colleges should be aware that the CDM regulations place new duties on employers (colleges), designers and contractors obliging them to consider health and safety throughout all stages of a construction project from initial conception to subsequent maintenance, repair and even demolition.

One of the new requirements is that colleges will be obliged to appoint a planning supervisor to oversee the design and preparation of the project in order that risks are avoided or minimised at the start, as far as is reasonably practical. The planning supervisor has a duty to produce a health and safety plan covering all stages of the project to include a detailed examination of risk management. The planning supervisor can, if necessary, be an employee of the college or may indeed fulfil a combined role with that of principal contractor.

Colleges should be particularly aware that work must not start on site until the health and safety plan has been completed by the planning supervisor.

On the matter of project administration, the college must maintain a safety file of information about the project to enable anyone who may require information to comply with the requirements imposed on them to have ready access to such information. This file must be passed on to any future owners of a college property upon its disposal.

Since breaches of health and safety regulations, including the CDM Regulations, can lead to prosecution and conviction, it is essential that proper advice is sought on this issue and those mentioned above where appropriate.

g. Performance Bonds

On major construction projects, a performance bond is used as a guarantee of monies for the client, usually from the funder of the contractor. The bond, which may equate to 10 per cent of the contract sum, is made out to the client and guards against non-performance and/or serious default by the contractor. The bond will be called by the client in the event of the contractor becoming insolvent during the currency of the contract.

GUIDANCE SUMMARY

- Colleges should seek expert professional advice to help determine the most appropriate form of contract.

4 SELECTING TENDERERS

4.1   In selecting tenderers for works contracts, the aim is to ensure the achievement of economic, efficient and effective competition for services from a fully representative sample of interested and capable contractors. This needs to be achieved by way of procedures which treat contractors evenly whilst meeting any public sector obligations with regard to procurement such as relevant EU directives.

4.2   In general, contractors should be selected to tender on the basis of relevant experience and appropriate expertise. If a college is uncertain about its precise needs, it may be necessary to engage the services of a specialist consultant to provide procurement advice. Pre-qualification tenders are also commonly used in works contracts and their use is described later in this chapter.

4.3   A major issue for colleges especially in connection with minor capital works procurement is whether to opt for a negotiated single tender bid, as opposed to a competitive tendering strategy. In practice, competition is generally viewed as the more cost-effective by purchasers of works services.

What form of tender procedures are available?

How should contractors' records be maintained?

Single Tender

4.4   Single tendering is the appointment of a contractor without testing the market through competition. Although this approach is not favoured by the public sector, it may be an appropriate tendering strategy if a contractor has undertaken earlier work for the college and has built up a degree of knowledge and experience that is unique. Alternatively single tendering may be appropriate for all commissions below a threshold to be set by each college.

4.5   Recommendation – single tender is not appropriate for the engagement of contractors unless the value of the contract is less than, say, £2,500 or it can be demonstrated clearly on value for money grounds that a previous contractor should be re-appointed or a contract extended. Care should be taken to avoid awarding a series of single tender projects to the same contractor where the cumulative total, in any one year, becomes significant (say, £20,000 or more).

Open Tendering

4.6   This entails selecting a firm by general advertisement and inviting contractors to apply for tender documents. Open tendering is often referred to as indiscriminate tendering. This is not widely favoured by the public sector because the cost of tendering in relation to the likelihood of success can be very high and the quality of responses can suffer as a result, that is, some contractors will not expect to succeed. The cost to the college of dealing with a large number of enquiries and tenders can also be very high.

4.7   Recommendation – open tendering is not appropriate for the majority of works contract appointments although it can be beneficial on large projects or where this is permissible to meet the EU Works Directive.

Ad Hoc Selection

4.8   Firms of contractors may be selected following the placing of an advertisement or from prior knowledge. Typically, a short list will be prepared from those responding to an initial request for expressions of interest. The short-listed contractors will then be asked to submit a detailed proposal for evaluation by the college. This is, in essence, a two-stage tendering process.

4.9   Recommendation – this can be a useful approach to continually test the market although it may not lead to any continuity of works from tried-and-tested contractors.

Select from Approved Lists

4.10   If an approved list is used, colleges should develop detailed guidance on the credentials for approving and remaining on the list. Where an approved list has been inherited from a local education authority, colleges should review it in accordance with their developing procedures.

4.11   Selecting contractors on a random basis or by rotation from an approved list is unlikely to result in value for money being obtained except for the most routine of commissions. Despite the above comments, the use of approved lists is very common in the public sector, the main advantage being that the need to advertise each commission is removed.

4.12   Recommendation – this tendering strategy can provide value for money so long as the list is kept up to date and presence on the list requires contractors to pass an appropriate quality test related to matters such as relevant experience. When considering relevant experience, colleges should pay specific attention to the number of contracts awarded by other colleges for similar work.

Maintenance of Contractors' Records

4.13   A record of all contractors invited to tender for works should be maintained. This will assist colleges in developing and sustaining an accurate and up-to-date listing of contractors. The information to be recorded should include:

- name, address, contact
- turnover
- services offered and financial limits
- services provided to colleges
- associated companies – specific areas of interest
- notices of previous invitations to tender and any current commissions
- performance rating.

Number of Tenderers

4.14   The number of tenderers sought for works contracts will vary in accordance with the scale of the contract. For small capital works, single tenders or a small number of tenderers may be appropriate. However, for major capital projects, formal tender procedures will be necessary.

4.15   As a general principle, the higher the value of the works, the greater the number of organisations that should be invited to tender. However, if the contract is likely to be above the EU Works Directive threshold, special rules will apply.

4.16   Account has been taken of good practice in the college sector and other business sectors and it is felt reasonable to set a series of tendering thresholds as shown in the table below. It is important to note that the thresholds are broadly applicable irrespective of the size of the college.

Value of Works	Type and Number of Tenderers
Up to £2,500	At college's discretion – single tenders may be appropriate
£2,500 – £10,000	Prepare written specification – invite minimum of 3 written quotations.
£10,000 – £50,000	Prepare detailed specification sealed bids from between 3 – 6 tenderers
£50,000 – EU limit	Two-stage tendering – pre-qualification then prepare detailed specification. Request sealed bids from between 4 – 6 tenderers
EU limit +	Refer to EU guidance.

Note: EU limit for Works Contracts is set at 5 million ECU (approximately £3.95 million) at the date of publication of the good practice guide (November 1995). This limit varies from time to time and colleges and their professional advisers should take care to ensure that they are aware of the current limits before determining the tender strategy for a project.

GUIDANCE SUMMARY

- Single tender – appropriate for small projects (say, less than £2,500) or where specialist knowledge and experience exists giving contractors a competitive advantage.

- Open tendering – not generally recommended. Can place undue burden on college and contractors.

- Ad hoc selection – useful means of testing market if two-stage tendering used.

- Approved lists – appropriate for routine work. List must be regularly reviewed (at least once a year).

- Length of tender list should increase with value of project up to a maximum of between 6 and 8.

- Two-stage tendering can be of great benefit to both college and contractor.

- The college should ensure that no conflict of interest occurs and that the appropriate steps are taken to avoid any impact on the tender process.

- Colleges should ensure that decisions are properly and accurately recorded and held on file for future reference.

CASE STUDY

Where large quantities of repetitive works were required across the college's estate (in this case, roofing and electrical rewiring), College X first used their external consultants to provide a highly detailed specification for the standard of workmanship and materials. Tenders were invited from an approved list (with additional firms added after discussion between college and consultants) and potential contractors asked to break down quotations by building and provide method statements as to how they would meet the stated specification As a result, the college has been able to successfully mix and match the awarding of contracts to a range of firms according to price and quality criteria.

CASE STUDY

College Y has adopted a multi-faceted approach to the identification of contractors for undertaking minor works. For all external contracts, a combination of existing knowledge and specialist advice is used to identify specific contractors for individual jobs. The college's external advisers prepare a short list of potential contractors with references and recommendations. The college then consults a number of other organisations to finalise the list. These include both professional bodies and the local authority contractor hotline which is a complementary approach to identifying contractors for certain jobs. Quotations are then invited from the finalised list against the contract specification.

CASE STUDY

For many colleges it is important to establish good working relationships with a range of local contractors who can be called on for small scale or ad hoc routine works. College Z recognised that its works needs could neither be met by tendering every small job nor was there a sufficiently regular stream of work to justify retaining a large in-house staff. It tackled the problem by first drawing up a list of potential contractors, using a variety of local contacts (for example, reputable local architectural practices and the local education authority) to suggest suitable contractors. The college then drew up a specification of the types of work required and asked for quotations across a typical list of possible job types. The college now has a small team of local specialist contractors which it uses for small works, raising orders from each on an ad hoc basis. The college will re-tender the contracts on an annual basis to ensure it continues to achieve competitive prices for its regular work.

5 INVITING TENDERS

5.1   This section covers the procedures that should be adopted when inviting tenders for the appointment of contractors.

When should pre-qualification procedures be adopted?

What should tender documents include?

What instructions should be given to tenderers?

How long should tender periods be?

How can tendering 'rings' be avoided?

Pre-qualification

5.2   If the college has elected to pursue a competitive tender strategy, a pre-qualification process can help narrow down the field of potential bidders to a sample of those who are genuinely capable of meeting the college's needs.   A properly conducted pre-qualification process will ensure that all short-listed tenders have passed a certain quality threshold. Without it, the pursuit of the lowest tender does not necessarily guarantee the delivery of appropriate quality standards.

5.3   One further advantage of the pre-qualification process is that it makes the tender evaluation exercise for colleges that much easier by bringing forward bids from organisations or consortia having broadly similar and appropriate experience and competence.

5.4   A short list can be established by a variety of means including:

- advertising in trade press and other media seeking expressions of interest. The advertisement will need to be absolutely clear about the information sought from prospective tenderers in addition to describing the works contract in sufficient detail

- direct approaches to contractors who are known to be interested. Direct approaches can be made to supplement advertising or other means of identifying a prospective short list

- contacting professional institutions for a list of contractors with relevant experience in the area of interest

- from the college's own experience, the experiences of other colleges or from any existing approved list.

5.5   If the project value is in excess of five million ECU (approximately £3.95M) it will need to be advertised in the *Official Journal of the European Community* (OJEC). The procedure to be followed is highlighted on page 64 and the table overleaf sets out the thresholds for contract value at the time of writing (November 1995). Further information can be obtained from the Information Service Unit of the European Commission at the address in the Appendix.

Contract	Threshold	
	ECUs (Jan 1996)	Sterling (approx)
Public Works (eg, new building)	5,000,000	£3,950,464
Public Supplies	200,000	£158,019
Public Services (eg, commissioning of a project manager)	200,000	£158,019
The above thresholds come into effect from 1 January 1996.		

Tender Documents

5.6   It is absolutely critical that all tenderers are in receipt of the same information, whether written or verbal. This may necessitate reverting to some tenderers with supplementary information which has been revealed in discussion with another competitor.

5.7   Contractors must have total confidence in the tendering process and must believe that one bid will stand the same chance of success as another. Otherwise, the time and effort put into bids and therefore the quality of the submissions can be diminished.

5.8   To a large degree, the quality of a tender is dependent on the extent and quality of information upon which it is based. Care must be taken to ensure the information provided to contractors is as comprehensive as possible, making clear which elements are meant to be contractual and which are provided for assistance and guidance. In essence, tender documents must demonstrate clarity, consistency and completeness. The main items to be addressed include the following:

- instructions to tenderers

- general conditions of contract

- scope of work

- standards and specification

- the project, its location, size, procurement strategy and estimated value

- details of other members of the professional team where appointed

- proposed remuneration system (for example, fee payable on lump-sum basis, time basis, or percentage of value or some combination thereof)

- technical documentation for example, drawings, bills of quantities, schedules of rates

- contact point where queries can be raised

- address where tenders should be returned

- time and date for receipt of returned tenders

- address where additional documents or information can be inspected

- key dates including commencement and completion of works

- insurance cover

- administration procedures.

5.9   If, as is recommended, a process of value assessment is undertaken to aid the evaluation of competitive bids, tenderers should be made aware of the broad criteria that will be used by the college's tender evaluation team.

Instructions to Tenderers

5.10   Information to tenderers about arrangements for receipt, opening and recording of tenders, the policy on errors, and debriefs should be clearly distinguished from the formal tenders and should be produced in the form of 'Instructions to Tenderers' or 'Notice to Tenderers'. Tenderers should also be notified that the lowest bid need not necessarily be accepted without regard to commercial credibility of the tenderer or other discretionary elements. The overriding criteria should be value for money, taking account of economy, efficiency and effectiveness. Instructions to tenderers should include, amongst others, the criteria or arrangements for:

- dealing with late tenders
- accepting telephoned, fax or telexed tenders
- qualified tenders
- alternative offers
- receipt, opening and recording bids
- errors found in bids
- debriefing
- confidentiality of tenders.

Tendering Periods

5.11   It is perhaps obvious but nevertheless worth emphasising that the college should provide all tenderers with the same information at the same time.

5.12   As a result, all tenderers will be afforded the same timescale to submit bids. The time allowed for submission should be sufficient to allow site visits (if appropriate), the inspection of any restricted documentation on site, the opportunity to raise any questions and the time to prepare a submission.

5.13   For a contract carrying out works of a routine nature which are neither complex nor likely to raise any unexpected issues, a period of three to four weeks from the sending out of tender documents until the closing date for submission may be appropriate. A major capital project on the other hand may need considerable time to prepare. Whilst there are no set timescales for inviting tenders, the contract strategy adopted will have a significant impact on how long the tender period should be.   If the chosen route is traditional or design and build, then the contractor will need considerable time to plan and price the works. If the contract strategy is a management contract or construction management, the bid consideration is more concerned with the calculation of the desired level of profit margin.

5.14   One way of assessing an appropriate time for tenders in major works is to ask the contractors at the pre-qualification stage. Alternatively, a review of historic activities and the tendering processes adopted by other colleges (for similar projects) can act as a guide.

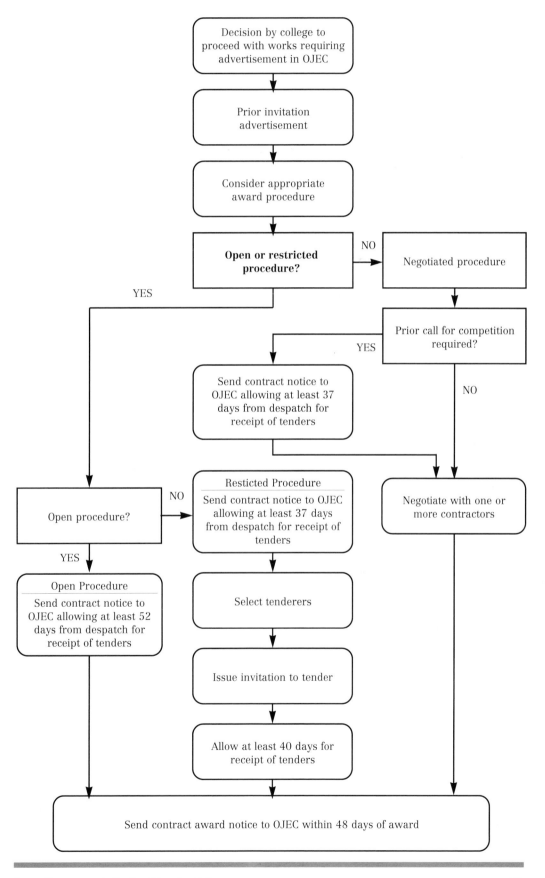

5.15 A more complex project where, for example, contractors may be expected to design and build a new teaching block might warrant a tender period of eight to ten weeks.

5.16 In addition, especially where a pre-qualification route has not been adopted, there may be merit in allowing a short period for clarification at the outset whereby contractors are granted an opportunity to raise queries and request further information. If any supplementary information is given to one tenderer, all others must be given the same information as soon as practicable thereafter if not simultaneously.

5.17 As a general rule there is little to be gained by putting undue pressure on contractors to meet onerous deadlines before they have been commissioned to provide a works contract.

Avoiding Tendering Rings

5.18 Tendering rings exist whereby some contractors collude to restrict competition and artificially force up the cost of contracts. While this practice may be difficult to stamp out, colleges can take avoidance measures to mitigate the potential impact of rings.

5.19 By liaising with counterparts in other colleges (and perhaps also schools and higher education institutions), estate managers may be able to obtain, for example, indicative costings for certain repetitive types of work. More formal benchmarking can also provide estate managers with guideline figures, whether absolute values, percentages or ratios, for a wide range of works and services.

5.20 Previous experience and knowledge of contractors can inform the process of judging whether tenders submitted by the same contractors for new work are done in a truly competitive environment. This stresses the importance of retaining full and accurate records of bids submitted by successful and unsuccessful tenderers.

5.21 The simple technique of altering tender lists from one commission to the next to ensure that new contractors are invited to tender should also contribute to an over-riding strategy that fosters competition. Tenderers should, however, continue to be selected with reference to such matters as relevant experience and expertise.

GUIDANCE SUMMARY

- Tender documentation should be clear, consistent and complete.

- All tenderers should be treated in the same manner.

- Avoid putting too much pressure to comply with tight timescales – quality of bids will suffer.

- One to three months is appropriate for contractors to prepare and submit most tenders – depending on the contract strategy.

- Take action to avoid tendering rings.

6 RECEIPT AND OPENING OF TENDERS

6.1   Equity and openness must be maintained throughout the tendering process.

In what format should tenders be received?

What procedures should be adopted when opening tenders?

How should late tenders be treated?

Tender Receipts

6.2   Tender documents should be submitted in such a way so as to ensure that the name of the company is not disclosed. The normal procedure is either to enclose a tender envelope with the invitation to tender or insist on tenders being submitted in plain envelopes showing no company markings. Return labels may be enclosed which indicate time, address, date of return and contract number along with a clear statement that contained within the envelope is a tender document.

6.3   Upon receipt, tender documents should be kept in a safe and secure place and must not be treated as ordinary mail.

Opening Tenders

6.4   Opening of tenders requires a degree of formality. It is recommended that tenders should be opened by senior staff not actively involved in the evaluation and award of the contract, thus ensuring the avoidance of any suggestion of impropriety. This may be an appropriate responsibility for the clerk to the college corporation, if one has been appointed. If college governors have any commercial links with contractors or consultants that the college may select, these interests should be declared and the individual concerned should have no part in the selection and evaluation of contractors or consultants and should not be present at meetings when these issues are discussed.

6.5   The opening of tenders should always be witnessed and clear records of tenders received should be kept. Each tender should receive a number in sequence to ensure that no other tender can be introduced at a later date.

Late Tenders

6.6   In general, there should be a presumption against allowing late tenders due to the potential for malpractice to occur. There are, however, certain circumstances where acceptance may be safe and equitable. These primarily relate to late postal tenders as follows:

- if posted first class and the envelope shows that the document was posted at least one day before the due date for the tender

- if posted second class and the envelope shows that the document was posted at least two days before the due date

- if the date stamp is difficult to read then the two day rule should apply

- if the envelope bears only the company's franking mark it should be rejected.

GUIDANCE SUMMARY

- Opening tenders should be a formal procedure.

- Clear guidelines should be given on the treatment of late tenders.

7 TENDER EVALUATION

7.1   At the heart of any consideration of value for money is striking the right balance between price and quality. Colleges need to be entirely open in their handling of competitive bids for works. An evaluation methodology that rationally considers competing bids for works contracts is therefore required.

How can a college carry out a rounded evaluation of bids?

What factors, other than price, should be taken into account?

Should a college enter into post-tender negotiation?

7.2   One such methodology is entitled value assessment which is consistent with *The Public Services Contracts Regulations*, 1993 and is equally applicable to public and private sectors.

7.3   Value assessment involves the derivation and use of a range of quality criteria to be used alongside a comparison of relative prices. It aims to quantify the unquantified so that competing bids can be 'scored'. The principal stages of a value assessment exercise are shown opposite.

7.4   The first task is to attach a weighting to the amalgam of qualitative factors. More complex works requiring fresh thinking and the application of a novel solution would warrant a relatively high weighting for quality and a corresponding low weighting for price. The table below gives some guidance to colleges in determining the right balance of weightings.

Nature of Contract		Weighting Distribution	
Category	Example	Quality (%)	Price (%)
Minor works	Redecoration, replacing electrical/plumbing fittings	5-10	90-95
Non-routine minor works	Security systems, fire protection, lifts	20-40	60-80
Major works	New block	40-60	60-40
Complex major works	New IT installation, new campus	40-60	60-40

7.5   Next, the college must determine which quality criteria are relevant and important to the works being commissioned and the relative weightings of these criteria.

7.6   It is advisable to include a commentary on the quality criteria to be adopted (where used) and their relative weightings in any tender documents.

7.7   Some suggested quality-related criteria are set out in the table on page 72 together with suggested relative weightings.

7.8   Before tenders are opened, the Tender Evaluation Team should set out on a Tender Evaluation Sheet the quality criteria, their weightings and the weighting attributed to price.

VALUE ASSESSMENT OF TENDERS

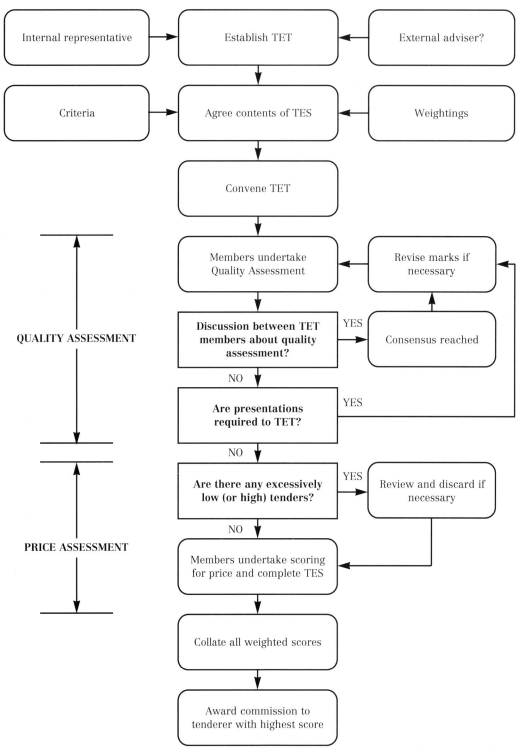

TET = Tender evaluation team

TES = Tender evaluation schedule

Source: Adapted from Construction Industry Council 'The Procurement of Professional Services', 1994

QUALITATIVE CRITERIA

Core Criterion	Issue	Suggested Weighting Range (%)
Experience	Reputation and experience	15-30
	Special competence	0-20
Technical Skills	Qualifications and CVs of key staff	10-25
	Special techniques	0-5
Management	Enthusiasm and commitment	0-10
	Communications skills	10-20
	Financial stability	0-10
	Quality assurance/Indemnity insurance	0-10
Implementation	Understanding of needs	10-20
	Logical and practical approach	20-30
	Management/control procedures	10-20
	Work programme	5-20

Undertaking the Value Assessment

7.9   Separate Tender Evaluation Sheets should be produced for each submission for completion by each member of the Tender Evaluation Team.

7.10   Each quality criterion could be given a mark out of ten by each member of the tender evaluation team following consideration of the tender submission and on hearing a presentation if appropriate. Differences in scores can be tackled by discussion until consensus is reached or simply by averaging out each member's scores.

7.11   There are various methods adopted in practice to score the price element in the evaluation exercise. One approach, in the first instance, is to discount any rogue bids which cause serious concerns about the quality and amount of resources likely to be made available by the contractor. A benchmark of perhaps 30 per cent below the average of all bids might set the limit outside which any bids will be discarded. At the other extreme, unduly high bids should also be discarded particularly if there is supporting evidence from the submission that the contractor does not understand the college's needs.

7.12   The next stage is to calculate the mean bid and allocate points. For all bids, add 1 point for every 5 per cent (or 0.1 point for every 0.5 per cent) below the mean and deduct points in a similar fashion for bids above the mean.

7.13   It should then be possible to complete each Tender Evaluation Sheet by multiplying scores by weightings to arrive at a total weighted score for each bid. The tender with the highest mark should be awarded the contract.

7.14   All sheets should be signed and dated and a summary sheet produced for audit purposes.

7.15   A suggested format for a Tender Evaluation Sheet, set out to evaluate bids for a works contract where price is deemed to warrant a maximum of 50 per cent of the total potential score appears on page 71.

Post-tender Negotiation

7.16   Post-tender negotiation is defined as by the Chartered Institute of Purchasing as:

> **Negotiation after receipt of formal bids or tenders and before the letting of contract(s) with those companies submitting tender(s) offering the best value for money with a view to obtaining an improvement in content in circumstances which do not put the other tenderers at a disadvantage, distort competition or affect adversely trust in the competitive tendering process.**

7.17   It should not be entered into without full justification by senior management within the college. This should take the form of a written statement giving the reason(s) which should be incorporated in the relevant project file.

7.18   There is no doubt that discounts can be achieved by post-tender negotiation although some purchasing bodies believe it can be self-defeating. Once a college acquires a reputation for conducting post-tender negotiation on a regular basis, it is conceivable that contractors will tend to bid higher thus allowing scope to concede a margin.

7.19   Nevertheless, many public (and private) sector organisations engage in this activity with the aim of reducing day rates, the overall price quoted or increasing the projected level of input while maintaining the price as a constant.

7.20   It is recommended that any post-tender negotiation is conducted by (or with the aid of) an individual accustomed to negotiating the terms of contracts with a view to securing better value for money.

7.21   There is a risk that post-tender negotiations can expose a college to accusations of impropriety. It is suggested, therefore, that such negotiation is only entered into with a preferred contractor rather than all parties on a short list.

GUIDANCE SUMMARY

- Securing value for money requires an assessment of both quality and price.

- Value assessment allows quality criteria to be rationally addressed.

- Post-tender negotiation is recommended provided one or more tenderer is not put in a more advantageous position than others.

MODEL TENDER EVALUATION SHEET

Project name

Project quality rating   50%

Project price rating   50%

Tenderer

Assessor

Criteria	Weighting	Score	Weighted score
QUALITY:			
Reputation and experience	8	8	64
Special experience	2	7	14
Qualifications and CVs of key staff	6	6	36
Special techniques	0	0	0
Enthusiasm and commitment	4	9	36
Communication skills	6	8	48
Compatibility	4	5	20
Financial stability	3	4	12
Quality assurance/indemnity insurance	2	8	16
Understanding of needs	7	6	42
Approach	4	5	20
Management/control procedures	2	2	4
Work programme	2	4	8
TOTAL	50(%)		320
PRICE (brought forward)	50(%)		290
Total weighted score			**610**

Signed   Dated

8 AWARDING CONTRACTS AND DECLINING TENDERS

8.1   Having completed the evaluation of competitive bids, the college will have identified the tender that represents best value for money overall. College management should be totally satisfied with the rationale behind the decision since it may well be that all tenderers, including the successful party, will wish to enter into dialogue.

8.2   It is appropriate to discuss the strengths and weaknesses of bids with tenderers if asked since this can serve to improve the contractor's understanding of the college's needs and perhaps better prepare them for a subsequent bid.

8.3   Once the preferred tenderer has been identified but before the contract has been entered into, references should be taken up to confirm the contractor's competence and performance on previous contracts. Where a short list (of perhaps 3 or 4 contractors) has been derived, it may be appropriate to obtain references for all contractors on the short list to aid the final selection process.

How should contracts be awarded?

What should a contract contain?

Is it necessary to give unsuccessful tenderers any further information?

Awarding Contracts

8.4   A contract should be entered into detailing the responsibilities and duties of the parties. Since the posting of an acceptance triggers the creation of a binding contract, it is important that the following issues are considered:

- time limit for acceptance of offer

- potential ambiguities or lack of critical data

- the outcome of any post-tender negotiation or agreed amendments made during evaluation.

8.5   A contract document package can be produced for signature by both parties. It should contain:

- a method statement or specification of the work required

- the arrangements for performance monitoring

- the contract containing details of responsibilities and duties of the parties.

8.6   Although an instruction to proceed or letter of intent can be issued under certain circumstances when, for example, there is an urgent need to appoint a contractor, it is recommended that the formal award of the contract should be accomplished by means of a properly executed contract. For major capital works, legal advice should be sought if in doubt or, alternatively, matters should be delayed until the comprehensive contract documentation is ready for signature.

8.7   As a minimum, an instruction to proceed should include:

- a description of the works or services required and the maximum amount to be spent fulfilling the instruction

- a description of all outstanding matters on which agreement remains to be reached

- the basis of payment for the work to be undertaken in the event that the contract is not entered into.

Declining Tenders

8.8   Unsuccessful tenderers should be informed as soon as practicable after the Tender Evaluation Team has made a decision.

8.9   Both unsuccessful tenderers and the successful party should be sent a schedule of the bids submitted (from lowest to highest price) together with a list of the contractors that submitted tenders (in alphabetical order). By doing so, bids will not be directly associated with contractors. This information, when combined with any information gleaned from dialogue with the college, will hopefully result in more competitive bids being submitted in the future.

GUIDANCE SUMMARY

- Contract awards should clearly identify responsibilities and duties.

- Legal agreements, where appropriate, should be concluded before works commence.

- Unsuccessful tenderers should be notified quickly, told of the other firms on the tender list and the level of bids.

9 RECORDING RECOMMENDATIONS

9.1   The potential complexity of the decision-making process, particularly when a broad spectrum of qualitative factors is used, means that colleges should maintain a permanent record of the steps taken to evaluate bids.

What sort of records should be kept following selection decisions?

9.2   While the Tender Evaluation Sheets constitute a critical element in the audit trail, they can usefully be supplemented by a written commentary on the strengths and weaknesses of each tenderer/submission and the principal reasons why the successful tenderer was chosen. These items and a summary sheet of scores for each tenderer should be retained together on the project file.

9.3   In addition to meeting the requirements of a college to be accountable, the recording of recommendations can assist the individual responsible for managing the contract if he or she was not a member of the Tender Evaluation Team.

9.4   Depending on the levels of delegated authority in place, it may be necessary to submit a report to senior management and/or the college's property committee (or similar) on the tendering and selection processes. Any such reports should be marked 'restricted' and contain, as a minimum:

- an outline of the project including how it fits in with wider objectives

- details of the bids submitted

- rationale for selecting the preferred tenderer.

9.5   The report might also address the reason(s) why external contractors were appointed in favour of in-house resources and the arrangements for working with and monitoring the contractor.

GUIDANCE SUMMARY

- Constructive dialogue with unsuccessful tenderers can be in the interests of clients, consultants and contractors.

- Contract documentation should be completed prior to commencement of the work.

- Project files should contain a written record of the selection process and the rationale for the decisions taken.

10 PERFORMANCE MONITORING

10.1   Colleges cannot claim to be securing value for money from the use of contractors unless they implement a system of performance monitoring of the works being provided.

What does the assessment of value for money involve?

How can performance measures be used to assess value for money?

10.2   The three aspects of value for money (economy, efficiency and effectiveness) must be achieved in harmony and the extent to which each is being achieved can only be assessed by the use of performance measures.

10.3   The inter-relationship of economy, efficiency and effectiveness is shown below. It can be seen that the achievement of maximum economy is allied to the procurement process. While efficiency can be measured during the course of the works contract, it is quite possible that the effectiveness of a contract can only be measured after the work has been completed.

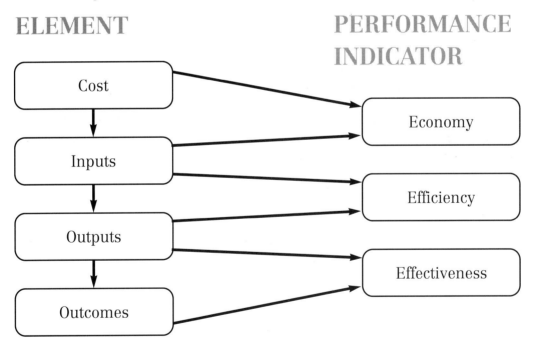

ELEMENT | PERFORMANCE INDICATOR

Cost → Inputs → Outputs → Outcomes

Economy / Efficiency / Effectiveness

Definitions

Economy: The practice of thrift and good housekeeping. Economical purchasing is acquiring resources of the desired quality at lowest cost. An appropriate performance indicator might be the construction cost of a new building per m^2 of gross or useable area.

Efficiency: The ratio of inputs to outputs. An efficient operation obtains maximum output for a given input or uses minimum input for a given output. Running costs per m^2 and building efficiency ratios (net to gross area) could be used as performance indicators.

Effectiveness: Ensuring that the desired outputs are achieved. Effectiveness can be assessed by conducting 'post project evaluations' with the aid of users of accommodation.

10.4 The following section deals with the monitoring of performance both during and after a contract has been awarded.

10.5 Ideally, quantitative and qualitative performance measures should be used. There can be advantage in discussing and agreeing performance measures with the contractor at the start of the work. Agreement should also be reached (and embodied in the project plan) on how performance will be monitored.

10.6 Performance monitoring might be by way of:

- on-site inspections and meetings
- written reports from the contractor
- percentage of works complete
- progress against plan.

10.7 In some circumstances, and in design and build contracts in particular where the college has no direct contractual or management links with the professional team, it may be appropriate to appoint a consultant quantity surveyor to assess the progress of works on site and to validate certificates for payment.

10.8 Other circumstances where it may be appropriate to appoint a consultant quantity surveyor may include:

- complex projects where cost control is critical
- where colleges have limited internal skills to monitor projects
- where there are significant negotiations with contractors over variation
- where the design team is appointed by the contractor and independent cost advice is sought
- where feasibility studies are to be undertaken.

10.9 Feedback on performance, from whatever source, should be in a format and to a timescale that enables the college to readily gauge achievement against targets.

10.10 Colleges should treat in-house works 'contractors' in a similar manner. The college needs to be satisfied that value for money has been achieved. Only then can the college decide the most appropriate balance in the use of in-house direct labour and external contractors.

10.11 Although this section is entitled 'Performance Monitoring', the act of monitoring performance is an integral element of the effective management of the contractor. This chapter, therefore, concludes with a brief synopsis of some of the principal problems that can arise in the appointment and monitoring of contractors.

10.12 Typical problems arising during and after the use of contractors, along with the causes of some problems, are as follows:

- poor specification of works

- inadequate pre-planning

- inadequate time for contractor to bid

- poor collaboration between client and contractor

- inadequately defined (or absence of) project plan

- uncertainty about whether contractor is committing the agreed level of resources

- appointing in-house project managers who have neither the time nor the expertise to get the best out of the contractor

- failure to work closely with contractors. This can pre-empt potential difficulties and keep the project on its critical path

- unclear allocation of responsibilities between design consultants and contractors, particularly with regard to mechanical and electrical services

- inadequate control over late changes requested by the users or architect and inadequate evaluation of their consequences for cost and timescale.

We have summarised a number of performance indicators that may be appropriate for monitoring works contracts in the table below:

POSSIBLE PERFORMANCE INDICATORS

PERFORMANCE INDICATOR	COMMENT
During construction phase	
Compliance with client's instructions	How quickly are they enacted?
Achievement against milestones	Can be cost or output oriented
Frequency of feedback	Regularity of written and verbal reporting
Nature and extent of disturbance to academic activities	Necessitates involvement of users
Cost against budget	
After completion	
Productivity	Requires derivation of output measures (for academic and non-academic activities)
Satisfaction of users	Post project evaluation to be carried out
Running costs per m^2 or per occupant	

GUIDANCE SUMMARY

- Performance monitoring procedures should be built into any project plan.

- Make contractor aware of performance measures to be used.

- Ideally, use a combination of quantitative and qualitative criteria to assess performance.

- Contractors should be proactively managed to extract maximum value.

11 RISK ASSESSMENT AND MANAGEMENT

11.1   It is essential for colleges to identify risks associated with building-related projects and then manage these risks by, for example, transferring them to another party.

11.2   Some risks will be capable of identification and perhaps quantification before a project commences. To cater for uncertainty and the fact that risk exposure can change throughout the progress of a project, systems must be put in place to manage risk effectively.

11.3   Although the transfer of certain risks from the college to other parties is to be a broad objective, it must not be blindly pursued. Value for money will not be obtained if risk is transferred to a party poorly positioned to manage that risk and if the increased cost of the risk transfer outweighs the benefits. If unrealistic risk is placed on the contractor, the client will probably suffer in the long run from project conflict, delays, claims and, therefore, increased costs.

What is Risk Management?

11.4   This can be defined as the planned and systematic identification, assessment, monitoring and control of risk. All well managed organisations attempt to manage risk throughout a project.

11.5   The stages of a generic risk assessment are shown on page 81 and described briefly below:

- identify what could go wrong
- assess how and when things might go wrong (for example, the impact on project cost or delays)
- monitor and control to ensure that the nature and level of risk exposure is acceptable by understanding this risk, establishing action plans to deal with risks and setting appropriate contingency allowances.

11.6   Colleges should consider employing specialist risk managers where complex projects are considered. This should enable management to be continually aware of the most likely and worst possible outcomes. With the benefit of such information, college management may be able to take early corrective action perhaps involving the transfer (or acceptance) of additional levels of risk.

11.7   In a project involving, for example, the procurement of a new non-specialist teaching building the risks could include, amongst others, the table shown overleaf.

11.8   A project manager with suitable experience (or a specially-appointed risk manager) should be responsible for compiling and maintaining a project risk register.

11.9   In addition to containing qualitative risk assessments (descriptions of the risks, when they will occur and their causes and effects), the project risk register can be used to derive quantitative assessments of the potential impact on time, cost and quality of the completed project.

11.10 There should be particular concentration on the most important risks and the quantification of their effects on the project outcome. A variety of techniques are available, such as probability and sensitivity analysis, to assist the college in establishing the worst, most likely and best possible outcomes. It is important to stress, however, that the techniques applied are only as good as the raw data fed in. As a

RISK ASSESSMENTS

Category	Source of Risk
Design Risk	Poor vetting of design team
	Poorly co-ordinated design team
	Use of new technologies
	Unreliable cost estimates
	Unsustainable project programme
Construction Risks	Bad site conditions
	Inaccurate data on services
	Inexperienced contractors
	Financially unstable contractors
	Ambiguous site management responsibilities
	No operating manuals/as-built drawings
Other Risks	Inadequate specification of needs
	Changing needs over time
	Interference with term-time activities
	Poor in-house management
	Ill-defined responsibilities
	Uncertainties over funding

result, a risk manager needs direct, constant contact with the design team and contractors to produce well informed risk assessments.

11.11 At the project appraisal stage, simple spreadsheets can allow the college to manipulate critical variables in cash flow appraisals to determine impact on net present cost or net present value. Specialist software is also available to assist the project manager quantify the financial impact of many potential (risky) events occurring simultaneously or in series.

11.12 Once risks have been identified and the total cost of risk to the college quantified, the successful risk manager will seek to reduce this cost while achieving value for money by continually appraising the costs and benefits of different options or 'risk responses'. The total cost of risk to the college can be thought of as a combination of:

- the cost of transferring risk, for example, by insurance
- the cost of reducing risk
- the cost of any retained risk
- the adverse risk arising from contracts with others (through financial claims by contractors and/or delays)
- the cost of the risk management function including consultant's fees.

11.13 In Section 2 of this chapter, a variety of contract strategies were discussed. An important issue for colleges in selecting an appropriate contract strategy is the allocation of risk between the college and the contractor. In the table below, potential contract strategies have been differentiated according to the allocation of price risk between college and contractor.

Contract Strategy	Risk Remaining with...	
	College	Contractor
Design and build	L	H
Traditional (lump sum, fixed price)	M	M
Traditional (re-measured Bills of Quantities)	M	M
Management contract	H/M	L/M
Construction management	H	L

Note: L – low risk   M – medium risk   H – high risk

PRINCIPAL STAGES OF RISK MANAGEMENT

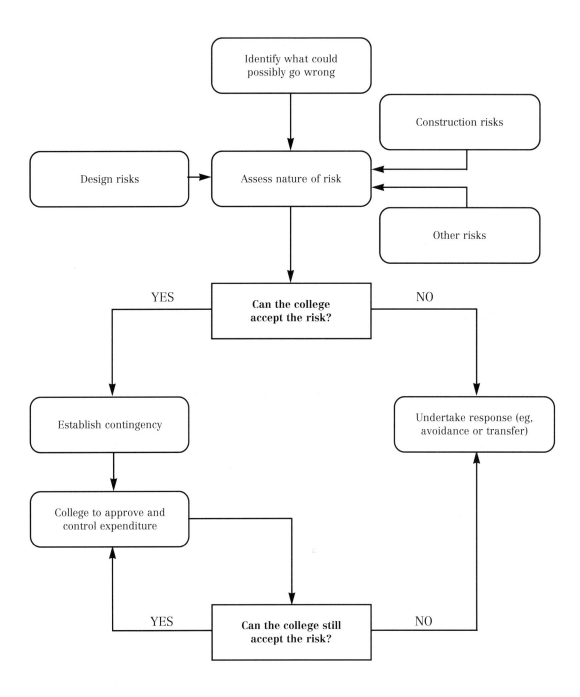

Chapter 5

PLANNED PREVENTIVE MAINTENANCE

Guidance is given in this chapter on the assessment, organisation and procurement of planned preventive building maintenance and the establishment of benchmark costs for building maintenance across the sector.

KEY ISSUES

1	Building Maintenance
2	Base Data
3	Links with the Accommodation Strategy
4	Organisation
5	Procurement
6	Benchmark Costs

CAUTION

- Ensure strong links between PMP, MIP and accommodation strategy

- Do not invest heavily in IT systems without fully appraising expected costs and benefits

- Avoid spending too much on a PMP as well as too little.

FURTHER READING

R Lee	*Building Maintenance Management*, Collins, London, 1987
RICS	*Planned Building Maintenance: A Guidance Note*, 1990
BSRIA	*Planned Maintenance and the use of Computers*, 1991
HM Treasury	*Working Group on Capital Asset Information Systems Report*, 1990
RICS (BMI)	*Condition Surveys*, 1988
BS 8210	*Building Maintenance Management*, 1986
CIOB	*Designing Out Maintenance Problems*, 1991
CIOB	*Managing Building Maintenance*, 1984
FEFC	*Guidance on Estate Management*, 1993

1 BUILDING MAINTENANCE

1.1 Building maintenance is a generic term encompassing three broad types of maintenance. In BS 3811, the following definitions are provided:

- planned maintenance – maintenance organised and carried out with forethought, control and the use of records to a predetermined plan

- preventive maintenance – maintenance carried out at predetermined intervals or to other prescribed criteria and intended to reduce the likelihood of an item not meeting an acceptable standard

- running maintenance – maintenance which can be carried out while an asset is in service.

1.2 Since preventive maintenance is normally planned, the term planned preventive maintenance can be used to cover the first two categories above.

1.3 A planned maintenance programme (PMP) is often associated with plant and equipment subject to mechanical wear but this chapter of the good practice guide is concerned with the building fabric.

2 BASE DATA

2.1   A PMP is an essential tool of the estate manager since it assists in the formulation (and monitoring) of an appropriate maintenance budget, schedule of resources, tackling backlog maintenance and managing or enhancing the value of colleges' assets. A link with the accommodation strategy of a college through the vehicle of a maintenance investment plan (MIP) must be created if the PMP is to operate in harmony with the strategic plan for the estate. Information is, however, the key to effective establishment and upkeep of a PMP.

What information is required to support a PMP system?

How should this information be manipulated?

2.2   To introduce an effective PMP, it is first necessary to produce an inventory of every building in sufficient detail to identify the components or areas requiring maintenance. Then, the college should establish the frequency of maintenance, the nature of the maintenance activity and the resource implications.

2.3   While the PMP for many items of plant and equipment is determined by regulation/legislation and the recommendations of suppliers, a PMP system for building maintenance can be less precise. Matters such as the consequences of failure and the past performance of individual components are important considerations in the absence of compulsion from legislation.

2.4   In general, much of the information that must be assembled to support a PMP will be of value to the college as an input to policy making and wider estate management. The individual with responsibility for preparing the PMP should have access to:

- the Hunter condition survey results supplemented as necessary by any other reports of condition

- full estate records including:

    - location, age and value
    - the strategic plan
    - construction details
    - building and site plans
    - original design criteria (for example, floor loadings, performance specifications)

- the college's MIP and maintenance standards (where these exist)

2.5   Account should also be taken of the following factors:

- climatic conditions, which can change dramatically between campuses for a multi-sited college depending on exposure and orientation of a building. Local factors such as proximity to neighbouring activities that emit waste should be noted

- user activities. If a college increases the demands placed on the estate by using it more intensively or for longer periods, an entirely different pattern of maintenance needs can emerge.

2.6   A condition survey is an essential pre-requisite of a PMP and should be supplemented by annual inspections. The effort required to prepare a condition survey is not significantly different from that required to enable a PMP to be produced. Colleges should use annual building inspections to update and clarify projected costings and other resource implications for the following financial year. It should be noted that the Hunter and Partner's survey was not a condition survey in the true sense and did not include the inspection of key building elements. Colleges should, and many have, commissioned their own full condition surveys including the intrusive inspection of key building elements as necessary.

2.7   This chapter does not explain the steps necessary to conduct a condition survey although reference is made to background material and authoritative guidance under 'Further Information'.

The Use of Information Technology

2.8   PMPs are frequently manually-operated and paper-based. One result is that such systems are often little more than 'bring-forward' facilities that flag up the date when a particular activity must be undertaken. They serve merely to keep a maintenance programme functioning and little attempt is made to analyse and proactively use the available information.

2.9   While the computerisation of a PMP is not essential, there is no doubt that it can be more effective for the larger college that wishes to integrate the forward planning of maintenance for its built assets in addition to all relevant plant and equipment.

2.10   Some of the benefits of a computerised PMP are set out below:

- improved (financial and managerial) control of the maintenance function

- rapid identification of areas requiring action

- enables operating budgets to be rapidly produced

- monitors stocks

- schedules labour force

- automatic preparation of works orders.

2.11   Computer-aided maintenance management can therefore enable colleges to use more effectively the information produced by a PMP. It allows the user to store and manipulate greater volumes of data more quickly and more accurately than might a manual system.

2.12   There is no simple rule of thumb outlining the circumstances when switching from a manual to a computerised system represents value for money. To assist the college in evaluating the advantages and disadvantages of systems, it should ask the following questions:

- how effective is the existing (manual) system in meeting objectives?

- what is the cost of the existing system?

- what is the likelihood of planned maintenance being outsourced?

- what is the current and anticipated workload of the maintenance function?

- what purpose would a computerised system serve bearing in mind that many off-the-shelf systems offer a variety of options?

PMP

2.13   As identified in paragraph 2.1 of this chapter, the PMP is an important management tool which can assist in the setting and monitoring of property-related maintenance budgets. It is, therefore, an important consideration in the overall budgeting process undertaken by the college. Beyond being a budgeting tool, it enables the college to plan its use of scarce resources. Finally, the PMP can assist a college in tackling a backlog maintenance problem in a rational manner and help prevent further backlog maintenance problems arising. Clearly, any mechanism which helps colleges avoid disruptive downtime by tackling actual and potential defects in a timely manner should be explored and implemented.

2.14   In its purest form, a PMP is a schedule of anticipated maintenance works to the college's estate. It is recommended that the schedule should look ahead for a period of no less than five years in detail. There is benefit in extending the PMP to 10-15 years to ensure that anticipated major repairs to new or recently-constructed buildings can be accounted for. A sample extract from one college's PMP which takes this longer term view is shown opposite.

2.15   The essential feature of a PMP is that building component failures are anticipated and appropriate measures are devised for their prevention or rectification. It may be appropriate to maintain spare parts or materials for the remedying of defects. This will depend on such matters as the frequency of occurrence (of the defect), the cost to the business of the college of a failure, the direct cost of retaining parts or materials and whether an outsourcing strategy for building maintenance is envisaged in the near future when the forward purchase of building materials might also be cost effective.

2.16   One means of assessing the nature of the PMP to be established is to carry out a risk analysis of the consequences of failing to take remedial or corrective action. Such an approach can allow colleges to rationally determine the right balance between planned and reactive maintenance.

2.17   Relatively sophisticated analysis is possible using simple spreadsheets to model the cash flows associated with the repair and replacement of building components. Maintenance profiles of entire buildings can therefore be derived which can help programme financial and human resources and materials.

2.18   Looking back at the past performance of building components (which may require colleges to access historic data retained by local education authorities) and by drawing on the recommendations of component suppliers/manufacturers, probability assessments can be made and built into the maintenance profiles.

GUIDANCE SUMMARY

- A PMP is only as good as the base data.

- IT can enable the college to more effectively manage the maintenance process.

A SAMPLE EXTRACT FROM A COLLEGE'S PLANNED PREVENTIVE MAINTENANCE PROGRAMME

Year number	1 £K	2 £K	3 £K	4 £K	5 £K	6 £K	7 £K	8 £K	9 £K	10 £K
1 Campus A.										
1.1 BUILDING 1										
1.1.1 Block A	2.5		2.5		2.5		2.5		2.5	
1.1.2 Block B	5	8	5	8	5	8	5	8	5	8
1.1.3 Block C	11	11	7	11	11	7	11	11	7	11
Subtotal building 1	**18.5**	**19**	**14.5**	**19**	**18.5**	**15**	**18.5**	**19**	**14.5**	**19**
1.2 BUILDING 2										
1.2.1 Block A	4	3		4	3		4	3		4
1.2.2 Block B	12	2	2	2	2	12	3	3	3	3
1.2.3 Hut						5				
1.2.4 Grounds & boundaries	1	1	1	1	1	1	1	1	1	1
Subtotal building 2	**17**	**6**	**3**	**7**	**6**	**18**	**8**	**7**	**4**	**8**
TOTAL A CAMPUS	**35.5**	**25**	**17.5**	**26**	**24.5**	**33**	**26.5**	**26**	**18.5**	**27**
2 Campus B.										
2.1 BUILDING 1										
2.1.1 Block A	6	6	6	6	6	6	6	6	6	6
2.1.2 Block B	9	1	1	9	1	1	9	1	1	9
2.1.3 Gymnasium	2	2			12	6				
Subtotal building 1	**17**	**9**	**7**	**15**	**19**	**13**	**15**	**7**	**7**	**15**
2.2 BUILDING 2										
2.2.1 Tower block	9	3	3	3	9	3	3	3	9	3
2.2.2 Classroom block	7		2				7		2	
2.2.3 Grounds & boundaries	0.7	0.7	1.4	0.7	0.7	1.4	1.4	0.7	0.7	0.7
Subtotal building 2	**16.7**	**3.7**	**6.4**	**3.7**	**9.7**	**4.4**	**11.4**	**3.7**	**11.7**	**3.7**
TOTAL B CAMPUS	**33.7**	**12.7**	**13.4**	**18.7**	**28.7**	**17.4**	**26.4**	**10.7**	**18.7**	**18.7**

CASE STUDY

College X operates a variety of computerised databases to assist in its programme of planned maintenance. One provides an information breakdown on a building-by-building basis summarising structure, fabric type, use, total areas, minor works and other upgrading/improvements needed. This data is then broken down on a room-by-room basis with information on size and condition together with room contents to form a complete asset register for the college. These sources of information are updated by the estates department by systems of regular inspection and following completion of individual projects. Further databases contain details of all cyclical maintenance requirements with names of contractors, type of service and renewal/repair dates to assist with performance monitoring and re-tendering.

3 LINKS WITH THE ACCOMMODATION STRATEGY

3.1   The PMP must be set in context and that context for a college is its accommodation strategy. Only by knowing the direction, in estate terms, that the college is moving in can it hope to secure value for money from its planned maintenance activities.

3.2   Teaching plans are subject to change which demands that accommodation strategies are kept under constant review. Those responsible for preparing and monitoring the PMP must, therefore, liaise closely with professional colleagues whose responsibility it is to keep the accommodation strategy up to date.

3.3   The link between an overriding accommodation strategy and the PMP is the college's policy on the maintenance of its estate. In the document entitled *Guidance on Estate Management*, the FEFC has suggested that this policy can be encapsulated in a MIP which comprises: '... a schedule which lists all its buildings and records the standard to which it has been determined each building should be maintained.' (p.16)

3.4   All three inter-linked documents (the accommodation strategy, MIP and PMP) must be kept in harmony. The achievement of this objective can be helped by maintaining an integrated database of information on strategic and operational property matters and by encouraging the free flow of information in both directions between those dealing with strategic and operational matters.

GUIDANCE SUMMARY

- The PMP must be developed and pursued in harmony with the accommodation strategy and MIP.

4   ORGANISATION

4.1   There is no generic model for the organisation of a college's building maintenance function, although there are certain activities which typically require to be undertaken almost irrespective of the size and nature of the estate.

What functions should the maintenance organisation perform?

What is the appropriate balance between in-house and contracted-out labour?

4.2   The PMP should integrate the overall maintenance function, the components of which can be described as:

Advisory

- maintenance standards
- planned expenditure
- dealing with backlog maintenance
- appropriate balance between in-house expertise and contracting out for procurement of works
- relative merits of repair and replace.

Organisational

- defining responsibilities and duties
- developing procedures
- devising information systems
- engaging operatives
- purchasing materials
- managing the workforce
- preparation of tender documents
- selecting contractors
- maintaining performance (of contractors and directly-employed labour)
- administering contracts.

Control

- identifying works required to achieve standards
- programming use of resources
- cost control
- quality management.

4.3   The above list assumes that both direct and contracted-out labour may be used.

4.4   Colleges should determine the most appropriate size and structure of their own maintenance organisation based on a consideration of the following factors:

- the likely volume of workload and its distribution over time

- the nature and complexity of the workload. Will the workload guarantee full and continuous employment? What is the likely balance between planned and routine work as opposed to reactive and one-off work? Is the complexity of the work likely to lead to the procurement of specialist skills?

- the location of the work. A multi-site college is likely to require a higher level of supervisory staff than a single-site institution

- the capabilities of the workforce. Are operatives capable of using discretion? How much control is needed to maintain quality?

- the organisational culture. Is the culture of the college one that is in favour of transferring risk and maintaining a small strategic core of support services? Does the college prefer to retain tight and direct control over all its support services?

- the managerial capabilities within the estates or facilities function. A large and varied in-house labour force requires particular skills of man-management to be vested within the college

- the relative costs of in-house and contracted-out services.

4.5   Colleges may have inherited a network of contracts for maintenance (and other) work from the local education authority. Alternatively, entire departments may have been built up from a minimal base to include a comprehensive multi-trade direct labour force.

4.6   Colleges should explore the relative costs and benefits of an in-house or external maintenance function. Decisions need to be made on value for money grounds (economy, efficiency and effectiveness) and with the benefit of full information on costs and benefits. For colleges, it will rarely be a choice between a complete in-house provision and completely contracting-out.

Direct Labour or Contracted-out?

4.7   The principal advantages of a direct labour organisation are said to include;
- greater control over allocation of work
- quicker response to emergencies
- improved flexibility
- detailed knowledge of estate can be developed
- greater sense of ownership of the solution and identity with college
- less perceived security risk
- no direct cost or time delay through having to tender and enter into contracts.

4.8   In contrast, the advantages of contracting-out include the following:
- specialists (rather than generalists) can be procured
- the college will not be paying for the inevitable idle time
- no need to provide dedicated support facilities (offices and workshops/stores)
- transfer of risk

- the market can be readily and frequently tested through competitive tendering.

4.9   Circumstances where contracting-out can be viewed as the preferred option include:

- where the specialist skills required could not be gainfully employed throughout the year by the college

- if a competent person is required by legislation to carry out a formal inspection; this applies principally to plant and equipment

- where the planned maintenance activity can be successfully integrated with other relevant work being undertaken by a contractor.

4.10   It is incumbent upon colleges to test on a systematic (and regular) basis that its chosen organisational structure and procurement strategy is offering best value for money and providing the desired level of service.

4.11   Even if a college adopts a strategy to internalise all or a great deal of its maintenance work, it should remain aware of the opportunities available elsewhere. This awareness can be fostered by liaising with other colleges and testing the market if only to compare the true costs of internalising the function with market prices. The establishment of an internal charging system whereby the full costs of support services are established and recharged to users (either notionally or in hard cash terms) will facilitate the cost benefit analysis exercise. The identification of all costs of in-house provision should be implemented to ensure a comprehensive evaluation of whether or not to outsource all maintenance activities. Relevant costs can include the salaries (for maintenance staff and managers), materials, transport, dedicated accommodation (for example, stores) and a proportion of college overheads.

4.12   The reader is referred to chapter 2 at this point which includes a commentary on organising an estates function within a college.

4.13   Colleges should be aware that the outsourcing of certain functions may not enable it to shed all the costs associated with the provision of these functions in-house. For example, some overheads will continue to be payable by the college irrespective of the source of provision of a support service. Nevertheless, the simple act of recognising this can enable colleges to utilise resources more effectively.

GUIDANCE SUMMARY

- Colleges should continually appraise organisational options to establish which delivers best value for money.

- When appraising options, the full cost of an in-house function should be identified and tested against other options from time to time.

- In determining the costs of in-house support teams, colleges must ensure that the costs of other overheads are properly allocated to this function.

CASE STUDY

When teaching departments request repairs or minor improvements at college X, they are required to submit one of a range of different requisition forms to the in-house estates team. These forms are designed for emergency/health and safety matters (which receive priority attention), routine maintenance, minor improvements, furniture/equipment and single projects over £15,000. The project application form includes a report skeleton to enable teaching departments to set out the need for the project and the objectives to be achieved, possible alternatives and general notifications to the estate manager and resources subcommittee. As far as minor improvements are concerned, individual departments are charged for activities which add value to their assets (for example, rewiring for IT use and provision of additional storage space).

PLANNED MAINTENANCE SYSTEM – THE PROCESS

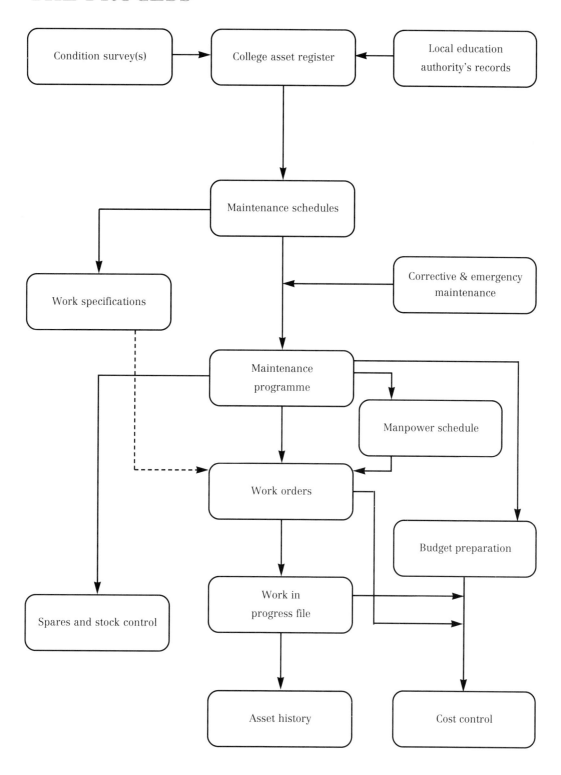

Source: Adapted from BSRIA technical note TN 1/85.1 'Planned Maintenance and the Use of Computers'. J Armstrong, February 1991

5 PROCUREMENT

5.1 Irrespective of whether planned maintenance works are carried out by internal staff or by outside consultants, a number of stages must be followed by the college. Where planned maintenance is contracted out, it is critical that systems operated by a contractor interface with those of the college.

5.2 The diagram opposite shows the principal processes to be followed leading up to the preparation of a works order and the recording of completed works and resources consumed. These are commented on below:

a. the Asset Register must identify separately each asset to be maintained and for which a forward maintenance plan is to be prepared. A well thought out coding system will allow rigorous interrogation at a later date to help monitor past expenditure and programme future work;

b. a maintenance schedule lists the tasks required and when they should be undertaken. This can be produced automatically to accompany a relevant works order;

c. the work specification is a detailed description of the tasks to be performed and their sequence;

d. a maintenance programme is created comprising a forward-looking allocation of resources. The programme aims to 'smooth' the demand for resources;

e. the works order is written confirmation (to the operative) of the task to be performed. The works order form should allow scope for feedback by the operative on such matters as the need for additional work or recommendations on changes in the frequency of works;

f. the PMP must be integrated with calls for corrective and emergency works. Budgeting for maintenance should therefore take account of likely calls for expenditure on both planned and corrective maintenance activities;

g. the work in progress file records all jobs that have been instructed whether planned, corrective or emergency. This permits day-to-day scheduling of resources to be undertaken and decisions on prioritisation to be made having regard to available resources. A regular review of work in progress files will enable management to establish whether any additional (part-time or full-time) resources are required to bring supply and demand more into line;

h. an asset history is a log of inspections made and works undertaken and their nature. It can help to identify where maintenance is inadequate, where serious consideration should be given to replacement and where over maintenance may be taking place;

i. the control of stock is important where planned maintenance is undertaken in-house. The control system can foster effective supply chain management and thereby optimise the college's own purchasing and holding costs;

j. budgetary and cost control is essential to secure value for money from a PMP. The comparison of actual costs against budget throughout the financial year will

Estate Management in Further Education Colleges

indicate whether (and where) resources are being effectively applied. If there are links between budget preparation and responsibility for the implementation of work then control will improve.

5.3 The terms of the contract with the external contractor will rarely determine the quality with which the PMP is implemented. Where a college elects to carry out works in-house, there is still a need for the preparation of a clear specification of work to be undertaken and the monitoring of performance against the specification.

5.4 A contract with an external service provider should be drawn up and managed in accordance with recommendations contained elsewhere in this guide (see chapters 4 and 6).

5.5 If a contracted-out strategy is to be pursued, colleges should explore the opportunities that exist to package the preparation and implementation of the PMP with other property-related support services. For example, there can be advantage in co-ordinating the conduct of maintenance, cleaning and security services because of their inter-relationship. Guidance on facilities management is to be found in chapter 3.

Performance Monitoring

5.6 Performance measures must be established to determine the value for money being obtained from the arrangement for conducting planned maintenance.

5.7 Precise measurements are difficult to make partly because there is no standard 'unit of production' in the building industry and partly due to the variety of conditions under which maintenance activities are carried out.

5.8 The Audit Commission suggested (following an audit of health service maintenance management arrangements) that a guideline of 4-5 hours per 1000 m^2 per week should be devoted to planned maintenance activity. This recommendation was made in the context of an in-house maintenance team. In practice, a more sophisticated blend of quantitative and qualitative measures should be used.

5.9 General guidance is given elsewhere in this guide on the performance monitoring of contractors and consultants (see chapters 4 and 6 respectively). In this chapter, guidance is given on the use of some measures particularly suited to managing maintenance activities.

5.10 As with all performance measures, they should be simple to calculate, understand and use. A mix of quantitative and qualitative performance measures is to be preferred.

5.11 Quantitative performance measures can be grouped as follows:

a. productivity measures:

      i. man-hours per job

      ii. estimated time compared with actual time for completion of job

      iii. total cost per maintenance activity (including wages, materials and all overheads)

      iv. standard hours of work produced (where calculated following work measurement exercise or from past experience) compared with actual time taken. It might be calculated that a particular job should take 2 man-hours but an audit of performance reveals that the job actually took 3 man-hours when last carried out;

b. planning efficiency

    i.   productive time compared with time worked. Another approach is to look at idle or lost time compared with total available time

    ii.   supervisory time (and cost) compared with direct labour time (and cost)

    iii.   extent of scheduling of activities can be measured by comparing the number of hours for which operatives are to be gainfully employed with the amount of time theoretically available. This can highlight over maintenance and poor forward planning.

5.12   Some qualitative measures that can be used are:

- frequency and nature of complaints from users of college accommodation

- disturbance to core business (for example, teaching activities)

- quality of feedback from operatives

- extent of suggestions made to alter programme to secure best value for money

- perceived quality of repairs by building users and by college estate managers.

GUIDANCE SUMMARY

- If contracting out, particular attention must be paid to securing feedback and interfacing information systems.

- Clear specifications and performance indicators should be put in place irrespective of who carries out the works.

6 BENCHMARK COSTS

6.1   Various studies have been undertaken which have examined, amongst other things, maintenance expenditure on educational buildings.

6.2   Prior to the incorporation of colleges, the Department for Education gathered and analysed revenue expenditure by further education colleges in accordance with various categories including building maintenance. The Society of Chief Architects of Local Authorities (SCALA) has produced an annual survey of buildings maintenance expenditure on various types of local authority building although the most recent report is dated 1992. In addition, Building Maintenance Information, a division of the Royal Institution of Chartered Surveyors, has produced one-off survey reports following an analysis of building maintenance expenditure on samples of higher education institutions.

6.3   All of the above studies reveal a broad range of figures reflecting such factors as:

- the nature of the stock being maintained

- the varying degrees of importance placed on maintenance by different institutions

- the divergent maintenance policies in place.

6.4   It is also likely that the value of maintenance expenditure in any one year is not a measure of the actual amount of maintenance work required but could be more a reflection of the amount of funding actually available. Without knowing the methodologies used in calculating maintenance expenditure, it is quite possible that the recorded maintenance expenditures are calculated upon different bases. For example, it may be that major upgrading work is included as a maintenance item by some institutions but excluded by others.

6.5   Following an update of previous reviews of maintenance expenditures to take account of fluctuations in building costs, evidence suggests that a figure within the range of £5-9 per m^2 of gross floor area per annum might be an appropriate overall maintenance spend. Data from previous studies has been updated to the third quarter of 1994.

6.6   The quoted maintenance expenditure range allows for both services and fabric maintenance together with an allowance for decorations.

6.7   Research has also been undertaken into the relationship between new build cost and maintenance expenditure for a variety of building types. For the university sector, data has been analysed over a period of 21 years for a university estate from which one can conclude that maintenance expenditure expressed as a percentage of new build cost is typically in the range of 1.0 – 1.5. This approach can be used as a rudimentary check to validate expenditure estimates derived by other means.

6.8   For further guidance on the use of benchmark costs, colleges should contact the FEFC's property services team.

Chapter 6
PROCUREMENT AND MANAGEMENT OF CONSULTANCY SERVICES

The purpose of this chapter is to identify and disseminate good practice in the selection and appointment of consultants to advise on matters relating to estate management and the evaluation of the services provided.

KEY ISSUES

1	Selecting Tenderers
2	Inviting Tenders
3	Receipt and Opening of Tenders
4	Tender Evaluation
5	Awarding Contracts and Declining Tenders
6	Recording Recommendations
7	Performance Monitoring

CAUTION

- Beware of unduly low tenders
- Consultants need to be properly briefed and managed
- Record decisions for appointments and rationale behind decision.

FURTHER READING

Association of Consulting Engineers (ACE)	*Advice to Clients on the Selection of Consulting Engineers*
Construction Industry Council (CIC)	*The Procurement of Professional Services, 1992*
FEFC	*Purchasing by FEFC Sector Colleges, 1995*
HMSO	*Constructing the Team, 1994*
HMSO	*The Government's Use of External Consultants, 1994*
HMSO	*The Public Services Contracts Regulations, 1993 (SI3228)*
Oxford Brookes University/ University of Reading	*Property Management Performance Monitoring, 1993*

RIBA	*Directory of Practices*, 1995 (updated annually)
RIBA	*Standard Form of Agreement for the Appointment of an Architect* (SFA/92)
RIBA	*A Guide to the Standard Form of Agreement for the Appointment of an Architect*
RICS	*Client Guide to the Appointment of a Quantity Surveyor*
RICS	*Form of Agreement, Terms and Conditions of the Appointment of a Quantity Surveyor*
RICS	*Agreement for the Appointment of a Chartered Building Surveyor*
RICS	*Selection and Appointment of the Project Manager*, 1995
FEFC	*Guidance on Estate Management*, 1993

1   SELECTING TENDERERS

1.1   Some of the guidance contained within this chapter replicates that given elsewhere in this good practice guide but is included to make each chapter as self-contained as possible.

1.2   In selecting tenderers for an assignment the aim is to ensure that the consultant chosen has both the ability and the will to carry out the job in a cost efficient manner in accordance with the conditions of tender including, in particular, adherence to price and timescale. In ensuring this, the college will achieve economic, efficient and effective competition for services from a fully representative sample of interested and capable consultants. This needs to be achieved by way of procedures which treat contractors evenly whilst meeting any public sector obligations with regard to procurement such as EU directives.

1.3   In general, consultants should be selected to tender on the basis of relevant experience, appropriate expertise and knowledge of the likely costs involved. If a college is uncertain about its precise needs, informal discussions can be entered into with one or more consultants. It will be found that many consultants are prepared to enter into dialogue since this will be perceived as an opportunity to promote the practice of the consultant while, at the same time, enabling the college to clarify its requirements.

1.4   Such meetings can, if handled correctly, allow the college to explore the capabilities and experiences of prospective consultants in an informal manner.

1.5   A major issue for colleges should be when to opt for a negotiated or single tender bid as opposed to a competitive tendering strategy. In practice, competition is frequently viewed as the more cost-effective strategy by purchasers of consultancy services. It may, however, be appropriate to opt for the single tender strategy when, for example, the market is restricted to only one or a very limited number of potential suppliers of the service. It may also be appropriate to adopt this strategy where the knowledge and experience built up by a consultant following previous commissions on behalf of the college results in the practice being well up the learning curve for the forthcoming commission.

What form of tender procedures is available?

When should they be used?

How many consultants should be invited to tender?

How should consultancy records be maintained ?

How many firms should be invited to tender ?

Single Tender

1.6   Single tendering is the appointment of a firm of consultants without testing the market through competition. It may be an appropriate tendering strategy if a

---

consultant has undertaken earlier work for the college and has built up a degree of knowledge and experience that is unique to the consultant. Single tendering may be appropriate for all commissions below a threshold to be set by each college.

1.7   Recommendation – single tender is not appropriate for the engagement of consultants unless the value of the contract is less than, say, £2,500 or it can be demonstrated clearly on value for money grounds that a previous consultant should be re-appointed or a contract extended. Care should be taken to avoid awarding a series of single tender commissions to a consultant where the individual value is low but the cumulative value is significant in any one year (say, £20,000 or more).

Open Tendering

1.8   This entails selecting a firm by general advertisement and inviting consultants to apply for tender documents. Open tendering is often referred to as indiscriminate tendering. This is not widely favoured by the public sector on the basis that where tendering is open to all firms the cost of tendering in relation to the likelihood of success can be very high and the quality of responses can suffer as a result. The cost to the college of dealing with a large number of enquiries and tenders can also be very high.

1.9   Recommendation – open tendering is not appropriate for the majority of consultancy appointments although it can be beneficial on large projects or where this is permissible to meet the EU Services Directive on Public Service procurement.

Ad Hoc Selection

1.10   Firms of consultants may be selected following the placing of an advertisement or from prior knowledge. Typically, a short list will be prepared from those responding to an initial request for expressions of interest. The short listed consultants will then be asked to submit a detailed proposal for evaluation by the colleges. This is, in essence, a two-stage tendering process.

1.11   Recommendation – this can be a useful approach to continually test the market although it may not lead to any continuity of service.

Select from Approved Lists

1.12   If an approved list is to be used, colleges should develop detailed guidance on the credentials for approving and remaining on the list. Where approved lists have been inherited from local education authorities, colleges should step back to review these lists in accordance with the guidance developed.

1.13   Selecting consultants on a random basis or by rotation from an approved list is unlikely to result in value for money being obtained except for the most routine of commissions. Despite the above comments, the use of approved lists is very common in the public sector and one significant advantage is the need to advertise each commission is removed.

1.14   Recommendation – this tendering strategy can provide value for money so long as the list is kept up to date and presence on the list requires consultants to pass an appropriate quality test related to matters such as relevant experience. When considering relevant experience, colleges should pay specific attention to the number of commissions the consultant has gained from other colleges for similar services.

1.15 The concept of partnering, which can lead to serial contracting, can be appropriate where follow-on stages to earlier commissions are likely to come about. If applied correctly, such an approach is not inconsistent with obtaining value for money. With regard to the commissioning of consultants, it may be appropriate, for example, to reappoint a planning consultant to progress a planning appeal where the same consultant was involved in investigative planning work on behalf of the college and has therefore built up a degree of special knowledge. Colleges should, however, generally avoid the use of consultants on a retainer basis unless there are clear and demonstrable benefits that the avoidance of competitive tendering is still securing value for money. By combining forces and using their enhanced purchasing power, it is conceivable that colleges might wish to appoint a consultant on a retainer basis who will service all colleges on the same terms.

Maintenance of Consultants' Records

1.16 A record of all consultants invited to tender for services should be maintained. This will assist colleges in developing and sustaining an accurate and up-to-date listing of providers of consultancy services. The information to be recorded should include:

- name, address, contact
- turnover
- services offered and financial limits
- services provided to colleges
- associated companies – specific areas of interest
- notices of previous invitations to tender and any current commissions
- performance rating.

Number of Tenderers

1.17 A significant amount of work commissioned by colleges is of relatively low value. Single tendering is therefore likely to remain a component of each college's overall tendering strategy. Each college should be clear about when single tendering is appropriate.

1.18 As a general principle, the higher the value of the commission, the larger the number of organisations that should be invited to tender. If the commission is, however, likely to be above the EU Services Directive threshold, special rules will apply.

1.19 Account has been taken of good practice in the college sector and other business sectors and it is felt reasonable to set a series of tendering thresholds as shown in the table below. It is important to note that the thresholds are broadly applicable irrespective of the size of a college.

Value of Commission	Number of Tenderers
Up to £2,500	Single tender may be appropriate
£2,500 – £50,000	No more than 6 tenderers
£50,000 – EU limit	6-8 for brief proposals, then 3-4 for detailed tender
EU Limit +	Refer to EU guidance

Note: EU limit for Service Contracts is set at 200,000 ECU (approximately £150,000) at the date of publication of the Good Practice Guide (November 1995).

GUIDANCE SUMMARY

- Single tender – only appropriate for low value tenders (say, less than £2,500) or where previous knowledge and experience would give a consultant a competitive advantage.

- Open tendering – not generally recommended. Can place undue burden on college.

- Ad hoc selection – useful means of testing market if two-stage tendering used.

- Approved lists – appropriate for routine work. List must be regularly reviewed (at least once per annum).

- Length of tender list should increase with value of project up to a maximum of 6–8.

- Two-stage tendering can be of great benefit to both college and consultant.

- The college should ensure that no conflict of interest occurs and that the appropriate steps are taken to avoid any impact on the tender process.

- Colleges should ensure that decisions are properly and accurately recorded and held on file for future reference.

2   INVITING TENDERS

2.1   This section covers the processes and procedures that should be adopted when inviting tenders for the appointment of consultants.

When should pre-qualification procedures be adopted?

What should tender documents include?

What instructions should be given to tenderers?

How long should tender periods be?

Is there scope to adopt less formal tendering procedures?

Pre-qualification Process

2.2   If the college has elected to pursue a competitive tender strategy, a pre-qualification process can help narrow down the field of potential bidders to a sample of those who are genuinely capable of meeting the college's needs.   In effect, a properly conducted pre-qualification process will ensure that all short-listed tenders have passed a certain quality threshold.   Without it, the pursuit of the lowest tender does not necessarily guarantee the delivery of appropriate quality standards.

2.3   One further advantage of the pre-qualification process is that it makes the tender evaluation exercise for colleges that much easier by bringing forward bids from organisations or consortia of broadly the same degree of experience and competence.

2.4   A short list can be established by a variety of means including:

- advertising in trade press and other media seeking expressions of interest. The advertisement will need to be absolutely clear as to the information sought from prospective tenderers in addition to describing the consultancy services required in sufficient detail

- direct approaches to consultants who it is known may be interested. Direct approaches can be made to supplement advertising or other means of identifying a prospective short list

- contacting professional institutions for a list of consultants with relevant experience in the area of interest

- from the college's own experience, the experiences of other colleges or from any existing approved list.

2.5   Colleges may also consider making use of the Department of the Environment's Consultants' Register (CONREG). Following the recommendations contained within the Latham Report (1994), a working party has been set up to consider, amongst other things, the establishment of a single register of consultants seeking public sector work based on CONREG.

2.6   If the project value is in excess of 200,000 ECU (approximately £150,000), it will need to be advertised in the Official Journal of the European Community (OJEC).

Tender Documents

2.7   It is absolutely critical that all tenderers are in receipt of the same information, whether written or verbal. This may necessitate reverting to some tenderers with supplementary information which has been revealed in discussion with another competitor.

2.8   Consultants must have total confidence in the tendering process and must believe that one bid will stand the same chance of success as another. Otherwise, the time and effort put into bids and therefore the quality of the submissions can be diminished.

2.9   To a large degree, the quality of a tender is dependent on the extent and quality of information upon which it is based. Care must therefore be taken to ensure the information provided to consultants is as comprehensive as possible, making clear which elements are meant to be contractual and which are provided for assistance and guidance. In essence, tender documents must demonstrate clarity, consistency and completeness. The main items to be addressed can include the following:

- service to be provided

- technical documentation – for example, drawings

- contact point where queries can be raised

- address where tenders should be returned

- time and date for receipt of returned tenders

- address where additional documents or information can be inspected

- key dates including commencement and completion of commission

- insurance cover.

2.10   Where the consultant is to be employed in connection with a building contract (perhaps as a project manager), further information might be supplied as part of the tender documentation such as:

- the project, its location, size, procurement strategy and estimated value

- details of other members of the professional team where appointed

- proposed remuneration system (for example, fee payable on lump sum basis, time basis, or percentage of value or some combination thereof).

2.11   If, as is recommended, a process of value assessment is undertaken to aid the evaluation of competitive bids, tenderers should be made aware of the broad criteria that will be used by the college's Tender Evaluation Team.

Instructions to Tenderers

2.12   Information to tenderers about arrangements for receipt, opening and recording of tenders, the policy on errors, and debriefs should be clearly distinguished from the formal tenders and should be produced in the form of 'Instructions to Tenderers' or 'Notice to Tenderers'. Tenderers should also be notified that the lowest bid need not necessarily be accepted without regard to commercial credibility of the tenderer or other discretionary elements. The overriding criteria should be value for money taking account of economy, efficiency and effectiveness. Instructions to tenderers should include, amongst others, the criteria or arrangements for:

- dealing with late tenders

- accepting telephoned, fax or telexed tenders

- qualified tenders

- alternative offers

- receipt, opening and recording bids

- errors found in bids

- debriefing

- confidentiality of tenders.

Tendering Periods

2.13 It is perhaps obvious but nevertheless worth emphasising that the college should provide all tenderers with the same information at the same time.

2.14 As a result, all tenderers will be afforded the same timescale to submit bids. The time allowed for submission should be sufficient to allow site visits (if appropriate), the inspection of any restricted documentation on site, the opportunity to raise any questions and the time to prepare a submission.

2.15 A commission for a consultant to supply a routine service which is neither complex nor likely to raise any unexpected issues might allow a period of three to four weeks from the sending out of tender documents until the closing date for submission. A more complex commission for which individual consultancy practices are expected to form consortia to design a new teaching block, for example, might warrant a tender period of six to eight weeks.

2.16 There may be merit in allowing a short period for clarification at the outset whereby consultants are granted an opportunity to raise queries and request further information. If any supplementary information is given to one tenderer, all others must be given the same information as soon as practicable thereafter if not simultaneously.

2.17 There is little to be gained by putting undue pressure on consultants to meet deadlines before they have been commissioned to provide a service when an objective should ultimately be to create a close working partnership between client and consultant.

2.18 There is no right and wrong time period to allow for the preparation and submission of tenders. Essentially, the time allowed should not be so short as to make the process rushed and therefore risk substandard submissions. Nor should the period be unduly long so as to delay the start of the commission. Normally, a period of between four and six weeks is deemed appropriate for the preparation of most tenders not involving a pre-qualification process. Two to three weeks may be sufficient time for consultants to prepare bids for routine work and short-term projects. This may need to be extended if the project needs to be advertised in the Official Journal of the European Community (OJEC).

Formal or Informal Tendering Procedures

2.19   There may be occasions when colleges might wish to pursue rather less formal tendering procedures than are recommended in this guide. For example, the selection of consultants following a written submission and presentation might be the preferred tendering procedure. Such an approach may be appropriate if the college's objectives include discussing practical solutions to a problem with prospective consultants. Irrespective of the particular procedures adopted, colleges must be satisfied and be able to demonstrate that the tendering procedure has achieved the objective(s) of the college and secured value for money.

GUIDANCE SUMMARY

- Tender documentation should be clear, consistent and complete.

- All tenderers should be treated in the same manner.

- Avoid putting too much pressure on consultants to comply with tight timescales – quality of bids will suffer.

- Four to six weeks is appropriate for consultants to prepare and submit most tenders.

CASE STUDY

College X actively tendered for the pre-build stages of major construction projects as well as the building work itself. Management first discussed and drew up general objectives and identified potential resources such as FEFC minor works, surplus land, etc. Tenders for consultancy work were invited by advertising in the press and appropriate professional journals to obtain as broad a spectrum as possible. From the responses obtained a short list of consultants was drawn up. Each practice was asked how they would go about meeting the objectives identified by the college and how the proposals could be funded. The exercise was found to encourage fresh thinking and innovation.

3   RECEIPT AND OPENING OF TENDERS

3.1   Equity and openness must be maintained throughout the tendering process.

In what format should tenders be received?

What procedures should be adopted when opening tenders?

How should late tenders be treated?

Tender Receipts

3.2   Tender documents should be submitted in such a way so as to ensure that the name of the company is not disclosed. The normal procedure is either to enclose a tender envelope with the invitation to tender or insist on tenders being submitted in plain envelopes showing no company markings. Return labels may be enclosed which indicate time, address, date of return and contract number along with a clear statement that contained within the envelope is a tender document.

3.3   Upon receipt, tender documents should be kept in a safe and secure place and must not be treated as ordinary mail.

Opening Tenders

3.4   Opening of tenders requires a degree of formality. It is recommended that tenders should be opened by senior staff not actively involved in the evaluation and award of the contract, thus ensuring the avoidance of any suggestion of impropriety.

3.5   The opening of tenders should always be witnessed and clear records of tenders received should be kept. Each tender should receive a number in sequence to ensure that no other tender can be introduced at a later date.

Late Tenders

3.6   In general, there should be a presumption against allowing late tenders due to the potential for malpractice to occur. There are, however, certain circumstances where acceptance may be safe and equitable. These primarily relate to late postal tenders as follows:

- if posted first class and the envelope shows that the document was posted at least one day before the due date for the tender

- if posted second class and the envelope shows that the document was posted at least two days before the due date

- if the date stamp is difficult to read then the two day rule should apply

- if the envelope bears only the company's franking mark it should be rejected.

VALUE ASSESSMENT OF TENDERS

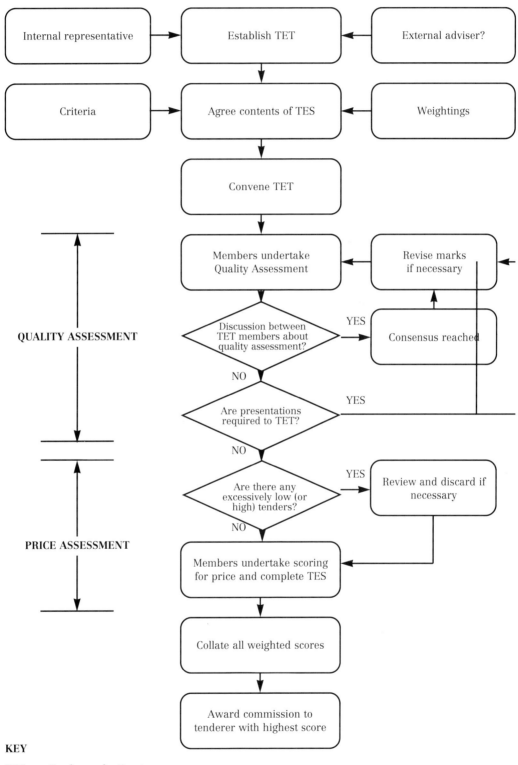

KEY

TET = Tender evaluation team

TES = Tender evaluation schedule

Source: Adapted from Construction Industry Council 'The Procurement of Professional Services', 1994

4 TENDER EVALUATION

4.1   At the heart of any consideration of value for money is the need to strike the right balance between price and quality. Colleges need to be entirely open in their handling of competitive bids for products or services. Beyond that, they need to be seen to be open. An evaluation methodology that rationally considers competing bids for consultancy services is therefore required.

How can a college carry out a rounded evaluation of bids?

What factors, other than price, should be taken account of?

Should a college enter into post-tender negotiation?

4.2   One such methodology is entitled value assessment which is consistent with *The Public Services Contracts Regulations, 1993* and is equally applicable to public and private sectors.

4.3   Value assessment involves the derivation and use of a range of quality criteria to be used alongside a weighing up of relative prices for bids. It aims to quantify the unquantified so that competing bids can be scored. The principal stages of a value assessment exercise are shown opposite.

4.4   The first task is to attach a weighting to the amalgam of qualitative factors. More complex commissions requiring fresh thinking and the application of a novel solution would warrant a relatively high weighting for quality and a corresponding low weighting for price. The table below gives some guidance to colleges in determining the right balance of weightings.

Nature of Consultancy Work		Weighting Distribution	
Category	Example	Quality (%)	Price (%)
Routine	Rating valuation, rent review, condition survey	L	H
Non-routine	Maintenance planning, organisational review, planning advice	L/M	M/H
Relatively Sophisticated	Project managing, new build, multi-disciplinary projects	M/H	L/M
Complex	Feasibility studies, value engineering	H	L

Note: L (Low)   - 20 – 40%
            M (Medium)   - 40 – 60%
            H (High)   - 60 – 80%

4.5   Next, the college must determine which quality criteria are relevant and important to the services being commissioned and the relative weightings of these criteria.

4.6   It is advisable to include a commentary on the quality criteria to be adopted (where used) and their relative weightings in any tender documents.

4.7   Some suggested quality-related criteria are set out in the table below together with relative weightings:

Qualitative Criteria

Core Criterion	Issue	Suggested Weighting Range (%)
Experience	Reputation and experience	15-30
	Special competence	0-20
Technical Skills	Qualifications and CVs of key staff	10-25
	Special techniques	0-5
Management	Enthusiasm and commitment	0-10
	Communications skills	10-20
	Compatibility	0-10
	Financial stability	0-10
	Quality Assurance/Indemnity Insurance	0-10
Implementation	Understanding of needs	10-20
	Approach	20-30
	Management/control procedures	10-20
	Work programme	5-20

4.8   Before tenders are opened, the Tender Evaluation Team should set out on a Tender Evaluation Sheet the quality criteria, their weightings and the weighting attributed to price.

Undertaking the Value Assessment

4.9   Separate Tender Evaluation Sheets should be produced for each submission for completion by each member of the Tender Evaluation Team.

4.10   It is suggested that each quality criterion is given a mark out of ten by each member following consideration of the submission and on hearing a presentation if appropriate. Differences in scores can be tackled by discussion until consensus is reached or simply by averaging out each member's scores.

4.11   There are various methods adopted in practice to score the price element in the evaluation exercise. One approach is, in the first instance, to firstly discount any rogue bids which cause serious concerns about the quality and amount of resources likely to be made available by the consultant. Rogue bids can be cross-checked by referring to schedules of personnel to be used and the time to be contributed by each consultant. A benchmark of perhaps 30 per cent below the average of all bids might set the limit outside which any bids will be discarded. At the other extreme, unduly high bids should also be discarded particularly if there is supporting evidence from the submission that the consultant does not understand the college's needs.

4.12   The next stage is to calculate the mean bid and allocate these points. For all bids, add 1 point for every 5 per cent (or 0.1 point for every 0.5 per cent) below the mean and deduct points in a similar fashion for bids above the mean.

4.13   It should then be possible to complete each Tender Evaluation Sheet by multiplying scores by weightings to arrive at a total weighted score for each bid. The tender with the highest mark should be awarded the commission.

MODEL TENDER EVALUATION SHEET

Project name

Project quality rating   50%

Project price rating   50%

Tenderer

Assessor

Criteria	Weighting	Score	Weighted score
QUALITY:			
Reputation and experience	8	8	64
Special experience	2	7	14
Qualifications and CVs of key staff	6	6	36
Special techniques	0	0	0
Enthusiasm and commitment	4	9	36
Communication skills	6	8	48
Compatibility	4	5	20
Financial stability	3	4	12
Quality assurance/indemnity insurance	2	8	16
Understanding of needs	7	6	42
Approach	4	5	20
Management/control procedures	2	2	4
Work programme	2	4	8
TOTAL	50(%)		
PRICE	50(%)	5.8	290
Total weighted score			**610**

Signed   Dated

4.14 All sheets should be signed and dated and a summary sheet produced for audit purposes.

4.15 A suggested format for a Tender Evaluation Sheet, set out to evaluate bids for a commission where price is deemed to warrant a maximum of 50 per cent of the total potential score, is shown on page 114.

Post-tender Negotiation

4.16 Post-tender negotiation, which is as applicable to the procurement of consultancy

services as it is to the procurement of works, is defined by the Chartered Institute of

Purchasing as:

'Negotiation after receipt of formal bids or tenders and before the letting of contract(s) with those companies submitting tender(s) offering the best value for money with a view to obtaining an improvement in content in circumstances which do not put the other tenderers at a disadvantage, distort competition or affect adversely trust in the competitive tendering process.'

4.17 It should not be entered into without full justification by senior management within the college. This should take the form of a written statement giving the reason(s) which should be incorporated in the relevant project file.

4.18 There is no doubt that discounts can be achieved by post-tender negotiation although some purchasing bodies believe it can be self-defeating. Once a college acquires a reputation for conducting post-tender negotiation on a regular basis, it is conceivable that consultants will tend to bid higher thus allowing scope to concede a margin.

4.19 Nevertheless, many public (and private) sector organisations engage in this activity with the aim of reducing day rates, the overall price quoted or increasing the projected level of input while maintaining the price as a constant.

4.20 It is recommended that any post-tender negotiation is conducted by (or with the aid of) an individual accustomed to negotiating the terms of contracts with a view to securing better value for money.

GUIDANCE SUMMARY

- Securing value for money requires a parallel assessment of quality and price.

- Value assessment allows quality criteria to be rationally addressed.

- post-tender negotiation is recommended provided one or more tenderer(s) is not put in a more advantageous position than others.

5 AWARDING CONTRACTS AND DECLINING TENDERS

5.1   Having completed the evaluation of competitive bids, the college will have identified the tender that represents best value for money overall. College management should be totally satisfied with the rationale behind the decision since it may well be that all tenderers, including the successful party, will wish to enter into dialogue.

5.2   It is appropriate to discuss the strengths and weaknesses of bids with tenderers if asked since this can serve to improve the consultant's understanding of the college's needs and perhaps better prepare the consultant for a subsequent bid.

5.3   Once the preferred tenderer has been identified but before the contract has been entered into, references should be taken up to confirm the consultant's competent performance on previous contracts.

How should contracts be awarded?

What should a contract contain?

Is it necessary to give unsuccessful tenderers any further information?

Awarding Contracts

5.4   A contract should be entered into detailing the responsibilities and duties of the parties. Since the posting of an acceptance triggers the creation of a binding contract, it is important that the following issues are considered:

- time limit for acceptance of offer

- potential ambiguities or lack of critical data

- the outcome of any post-tender negotiation or agreed amendments made during evaluation.

5.5   A contract document package can be produced for signature by both parties. It should contain:

- a method statement or specification of the work required

- the arrangements for performance monitoring

- the contract containing details of responsibilities and duties of the parties.

5.6   Although an instruction to proceed or letter of intent can be issued under certain circumstances when, for example, there is an urgent need to appoint a consultant, it is recommended that the formal award of the contract should be accomplished by means of a properly executed contract. It is conceivable that an open-ended instruction to proceed may act so as to create a contract for the entire commission. Legal advice should, therefore, be sought if in doubt or, alternatively, matters should be delayed until the comprehensive contract documentation is ready for signature.

5.7	As a minimum, an instruction to proceed should include:

- a description of the works or services required and the maximum amount to be spent fulfilling the instruction

- a description of all outstanding matters on which agreement remains to be reached

- the basis of payment for the work to be undertaken in the event that the contract is not entered into.

Declining Tenders

5.8	Unsuccessful tenderers should be informed as soon as practicable after the Tender Evaluation Team has made a decision.

5.9	Both unsuccessful tenderers and the successful party should be sent a schedule of the bids submitted (from lowest to highest price) together with a schedule of the consultancy practices that submitted tenders (in alphabetical order). This information when combined with any information gleaned from dialogue with the college, will hopefully result in more competitive bids being submitted in the future.

GUIDANCE SUMMARY

- Contract awards should clearly identify responsibilities and duties.

- Legal agreements, where appropriate, should be concluded before the consultant starts work.

- Unsuccessful tenderers should be notified quickly, told who the competition was and the level of bids.

6 RECORDING RECOMMENDATIONS

6.1   The potential complexity of the decision-making process, particularly when a broad spectrum of qualitative factors is used, means that colleges should maintain a permanent record of the steps taken to evaluate bids.

What sort of records should be kept following selection decisions?

6.2   While the Tender Evaluation Sheets constitute a critical element in the audit trail, they can usefully be supplemented by a written commentary on the strengths and weaknesses of each tenderer/submission and the principal reasons why the successful tenderer was chosen. These items and a summary sheet of scores for each tenderer should be retained together on the project file.

6.3   In addition to meeting the requirements of a college to be accountable, the recording of recommendations can assist the individual responsible for managing the contract if he or she was not a member of the Tender Evaluation Team.

6.4   Depending on the levels of delegated authority in place, it may be necessary to submit a report to senior management and/or the college's Property Committee (or similar) on the tendering and selection processes. Any such reports should be marked 'Restricted' and contain, as a minimum:

- an outline of the project including how it fits in with wider objectives

- details of the bids submitted

- rationale for selecting the preferred tenderer.

6.5   The report might also address the reason(s) why consultants were elected in favour of in-house resources and the arrangements for working with and monitoring the consultant.

GUIDANCE SUMMARY

- Constructive dialogue with unsuccessful tenderers can be in the interests of client and consultant.

- Contract documentation should be completed prior to commencement of work.

- Project files should contain a written record of selection process and rationale for decision taken.

7 PERFORMANCE MONITORING

7.1   Colleges cannot claim to be securing value for money from the use of consultants unless they implement a system of performance monitoring of the services being provided.

What does the assessment of value for money involve?

How can performance measures be used to assess value for money?

How can the college ensure a consultant genuinely adds value to its in-house activities?

7.2   The three aspects of value for money (economy, efficiency and effectiveness) must be achieved in harmony and the extent to which each is being achieved can only be assessed by the use of performance measures.

7.3   The inter-relationship of economy, efficiency and effectiveness is shown below from which it can be seen that the achievement of maximum economy is allied to the procurement process. While efficiency can be measured during the course of service delivery, it is quite possible that the effectiveness of a consultancy exercise can only be measured after the recommendations have been implemented especially if the consultancy is a short-term commission.

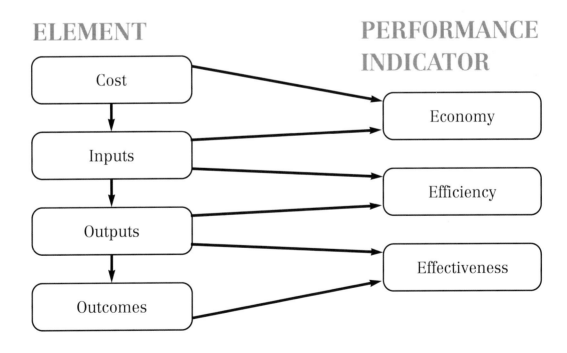

ELEMENT

PERFORMANCE INDICATOR

Cost

Inputs

Outputs

Outcomes

Economy

Efficiency

Effectiveness

Definitions

Economy: The practice of thrift and good housekeeping. Economical purchasing is acquiring resources of the desired quality at lowest cost.

Efficiency: The ratio of inputs to outputs. An efficient operation obtains maximum output for a given input or uses minimum input for a given output.

Effectiveness: Ensuring that the desired outputs are achieved.

7.4   The following section deals with the monitoring of performance both during and after a consultancy commission.

7.5   Depending on the nature of the consultancy, quantitative and/or qualitative performance measures can be used. Ideally, both types of measure should be used. There can be great advantage in discussing and agreeing performance measures to be used with the consultant at the start of the commission. Agreement should also be reached (and embodied in the project plan) on how performance will be monitored. Possible performance measures are shown below.

Service	Performance measure	Comment
Strategic property advice	Compliance with FEFC guidance Quality of report and analysis Consistency with teaching plan Compliance with project timetable	
Valuation	Compliance with instructions	Spot-check review of valuation of one or more assets
Professional agency	Duration for which college property on market Feedback on enquiries Proactive efforts of consultants Cost of maintaining unused asset Achievement of asking price/rent	 Could be outside control of consultant Scope for success-related fee

7.6   Performance monitoring might be by way of:

- on-site inspections and meetings

- written reports from the consultant

- feedback from users (for example, teachers) and others.

7.7   Feedback on performance, from whatever source, should be in a format and to a timescale that enables the college to readily gauge achievement against targets quickly.

7.8   Colleges should recognise that the use of performance measures for consultancy services is in its infancy and consultants might need some encouragement to work to relatively sophisticated systems of measurement and monitoring. Nevertheless, the point is worth stressing again that value for money cannot be ascertained in the absence of such systems.

7.9   Colleges should be prepared to treat in-house service deliverers in a similar manner. That is, the college needs to be satisfied it is securing value for money from property-related service providers wherever they originate. If in-house service delivery is to be properly evaluated, then the college must operate an internal pricing system which can properly identify the costs associated with the provision. Only then can it rationally appraise matters such as the most appropriate balance between in-house and external service providers.

7.10 On the facing page, some practical performance measures are listed against a variety of service areas.

Managing the Consultant

7.11 Although this section of the good practice guide is entitled 'Performance Monitoring', the act of monitoring performance is an integral element of the effective management of the consultant. This chapter, therefore, concludes with a brief synopsis of some of the principal problems that arise following the appointment of consultants and some rules of thumb in the use of consultants.

7.12 Typical problems arising during and after the use of consultants, along with the causes of some problems, are as follows:

- poor collaboration between client and consultant

- inadequately defined (or absence of) project plan

- selection of inappropriate consultants by reason of inexperience and lack of expertise

- failure to learn from the consultant

- uncertainty about whether consultant is committing the agreed level of resources

- appointing in-house project managers who have neither the time nor the expertise to get the best out of the consultant

- failure to act upon recommendations and thereby bring about the savings or other changes envisaged

- concern about the real value added in the context of in-house resources that could have been deployed

- failure of consultants to adhere to the terms of the brief.

7.13 To help colleges overcome these and other difficulties, some rules of thumb in connection with the appointment of consultants are listed below:

a. view consultants as a costly but potentially valuable supplement to in-house resources. This recommendation emphasises the need to weigh up the costs and benefits very carefully prior to any appointment or extension of a contract;

b. appoint consultants following a commitment to take action. This may sound obvious but, all too often, consultants are appointed to put off a difficult decision that management should take or prior to management signing up to a project;

c. clarify what is to be achieved by appointing consultants and how this helps the college meet its business objectives. It can often help if a brief scoping study is commissioned in the first instance;

d. set out the respective roles and responsibilities of the college, in particular that of the main point of contact, and the consultant. By doing this prior to the appointment of a consultant, college management will be obliged to address the best use of in-house resources. The implication of the above comment is that colleges should fully explore alternatives to the use of consultants such as exploiting in-house capabilities and learn from others in a similar business environment that have encountered the same problem. It is believed that significant scope exists to conduct benchmarking of the use of consultants within the college sector;

e. proactively manage the client – consultant relationship;

f. establish clear and detailed project plans to monitor the performance of consultants. The project plans should include project milestones, deliverables and mechanisms for feeding back progress against targets;

g. work closely with consultants. This can promote skills transfer, pre-empt potential difficulties and keep the project on its critical path;

h. formally evaluate the performance of consultants immediately a commission is completed using a range of qualitative criteria such as:

- achievement of cost and timescale estimates

- clarity of final report and recommendations

- quality of analysis leading to the recommendations

- practicality and achievability of recommendations

- value added to the college by way of, for example, immediate savings, improved processes, extent of skills transfer and better decision-making;

i. record the output from acting on consultant's recommendations and refer back to outputs predicted in the consultant's report for comparison purposes.

GUIDANCE SUMMARY

- Performance monitoring procedures should be built into any project plan.

- Make consultant aware of performance measures to be used.

- Ideally, use a combination of quantitative and qualitative criteria to assess performance.

- Consultants should be proactively managed to extract maximum value.

Appendix
USEFUL NAMES AND ADDRESSES

Association of Consulting Engineers
Alliance House
12 Caxton Street
London SW1H OQL
Tel: 0171 222 6557

British Standards Institution
2 Park Street
London W1A 2BS
Tel: 0171 629 9000

Building Cost Information Service
85/87 Clarence Street
Kingston upon Thames
Surrey KT1 1RB
Tel: 0181 546 7554

Building Maintenance Information
85/87 Clarence Street
Kingston upon Thames
Surrey KT1 1RB
Tel: 0181 546 7555

Building Research Establishment
Bucknalls Lane
Gartson
Watford
Herts WD2 7JR
Tel: 01923 894040

Building Service Research and Information Association
Old Bracknell Lane West
Bracknell
Berks RG12 7AH
Tel: 01344 426511

Chartered Institute of Building
Englemere
King's Ride
Ascot
Berks SL5 8BJ
Tel: 01344 23355

Chartered Institute of Building Services Engineers
Delta House
222 Balham High Road
London SW12 9BS
Tel: 0181 675 5211

Department for Education and Employment
Sanctuary Buildings
Great Smith Street
London SW1P 3BT
Tel: 0171 925 5000

Electrical Contractors Association
32/34 Palace Court
London W2 4HY
Tel: 0171 229 1266

European Commission Information Service Unit
8 Storey's Gate
London SW1P 3AT
Tel: 0171 973 1992

Facilities
MCB University Press Limited
62 Toller Lane
Bradford
West Yorkshire BD8 9BY
Tel: 01274 499821

Health & Safety Executive
Library and Information Services
Broad Lane
Red Hill
Sheffield
South Yorks S3 7HQ
Tel: 01742 892345

HM Treasury
Treasury Chambers
Parliament Street
London SW1P 3AG
Tel: 0171 270 3000

HMSO Bookshops
P O Box 276
London SW8 5DT
Tel: 0171 873 0011

Institution of Civil Engineering Surveyors
26 Market Street
Altrincham
Cheshire WA14 1PF
Tel: 0161 928 8074

Institution of Electrical Engineers
2 Savoy Place
London WC2R OBL
Tel: 0171 240 1871

Institution of Mechanical Engineers
1 Birdcage Walk
London SW1H 9JJ
Tel: 0171 222 7899

Institution of Structural Engineers
11 Upper Belgrave Street
London SW1X 8BH
Tel: 0171 235 4535

National Audit Office
157/197 Buckingham Palace Road
London SW1W 9SP
Tel: 0171 798 7000

RIBA Publications Ltd
Finsbury Mission
39 Moreland Street
London EC1V 3BB
Tel: 0171 251 0791

Royal Institute of British Architects
66 Portland Place
London W1N 4AD
Tel: 0171 580 5533

Royal Institution of Chartered Surveyors
12 Great George Street
London SW1P 3AD
Tel: 0171 222 7000

Royal Town Planning Institute
26 Portland Place
London W1N 4BE
Tel: 0171 636 9107

Surveyors' Publications
(Mail Order Dept)
Surveyors Court
Westwood Way
Coventry CV4 8HE
Tel: 01203 694757

Town and Country Planning Association
17 Carlton House Terrace
London SW1Y 5AS
Tel: 0171 930 8903

Printed in the United Kingdom for HMSO
Dd301928 1/96 C28 G3397 10170